JIMMY WHITE'S
SNOOKER MASTERCLASS

JIMMY WHITE'S
SNOOKER MASTERCLASS

Macdonald
Queen Anne Press

A Queen Anne Press BOOK

© Jimmy White 1988

First published in Great Britain in 1988
by Queen Anne Press, a division of
Macdonald & Co (Publishers) Ltd
3rd Floor
Greater London House
Hampstead Road
London
NW1 7QX

A Pergamon Press plc company

Jacket photographs —
Front: Richard McLaren
Back: David Muscroft

British Library Cataloguing in
Publication Data
White, Jimmy
    Jimmy White's snooker masterclass.
    1. Snooker
    I. Title   II. Poole, Charles
    794.7′35   GV900.S6

    ISBN 0-356-15583-8

Typeset by Leaper & Gard Ltd
Printed and bound in Great Britain by
Butler & Tanner Ltd, Frome

Contents

Foreword
by Jimmy White

The fact that you've picked up this book tells you something: you know about snooker and want to know more.

I've seen dozens of books on snooker, and they're pretty good, most of them. So why write another book? Good question. The trouble with most of the books on the market is that they spend a lot of time going over the basics.

When my friend Charlie Poole, a top amateur player and coach, suggested that we write a book together, we agreed it had to be different. It had to presume that most players had grasped the basics, were knocking in small breaks, and possibly even the occasional big ones, and wanted to get better. We thought we ought to write a book that would help you understand what every professional has had to learn the hard way.

How is it that we can build breaks that look so easy? How is it that the last two or three reds are often where we want them to make a clearance? How do we keep our cool (most of the time!) when the pressure's on and our bottle is really tested?

In *Jimmy White's Snooker Masterclass* we'll let you in on the tactics and tips that give you many of the answers you might not find anywhere else. There's a lot to learn about snooker, and none of us know it all. But I do know that your game will be streets better if you soak up the advice and put it into practice.

I can't guarantee that you can turn pro after reading this book. I can't guarantee that you'll make a maximum or a century (although I do believe that most 'average' club players have a 'ton' in them if they go about the game in the right way). But whether you're waiting to make your first 30 break, your first 50 or your first 100, you will find in the following pages advice that will open your eyes to parts of snooker that you haven't seen before. This I *can* guarantee.

Enjoy the book!

Jimmy White
London
March 1988

Introduction
by Charles Poole

ARE YOU READY FOR THIS?

There is no shot that a professional can play that you can't. Provided you know how. The difference is that, if you're trying to pot blue off its spot with the white in the D, the pro will expect to do it 19 times out of 20. The average for most amateurs would be six or seven times, or less. Why? It is because the pros have got their basics right. And when things begin to go wrong, they go back and check the basics.

Over the last 60 or 70 years, dozens of books have been published under the names of our leading billiards and snooker players. Most have at least one chapter on cue action and stance — and virtually all of them agree on the same principles.

I would imagine that most people who play snooker at all seriously have read at least one of these books. However, as I travel round the world, watching the top amateurs and club players, I am surprised that so few of them have used the advice and picked up really good cue actions. They lift their heads, they lift their cues, they persist with dog-leg cueing, they let their eyes bounce all over the place. The result is that they don't have a cat in hell's chance of becoming a professional.

Now, I realise that it's not everyone's ambition to be a top professional. Most of us have other jobs, or have realised that we don't have the time or the dedication, or we didn't decide early enough in life to take up snooker seriously. But I am sure that all players would like to find and attain their full potential. We all want to play consistently at the level that we can only reach occasionally now. With a little thought and work, this can happen — and more easily than you think.

Who is at fault in this business of poor cue actions? The players who can't be bothered to take notice? Or the authors for not putting over well enough the vital importance of the methods?

I have discussed this with many players and have done a lot of research on these books and found them both to blame. However, most of the fault is with the authors for not putting across strongly enough the importance of the stance and cue action.

We are not going to devote three-quarters of this book to the basics. We call it a *Masterclass*, and can promise you that we are not here to teach grandmothers to suck eggs. But, so that you can judge how far down the 'advanced' road you are, let's run through a checklist of the points in your action. Without these, none of the information will mean a thing, and you're not really ready to advance. If you're going to flick through this introduction, thinking you know it all, you might as well throw this book away.

1. Your stance depends on whether you are tall, short, slim or weighty. It is impossible to give a hard and fast rule about the way to stand.

Put your feet where they feel comfortable. Don't try to contort yourself into a style that you've read about in a textbook, or have seen a successful pro use. Stance is a personal thing, and all that Messrs Tall, Short, Slim or Weighty should have in common is that when they are down on the shot they must be completely comfortable and at ease.

You should not feel strain on any part of the body, and the legs and body must be perfectly still and balanced as you play the shot. If you feel awkward, move until you feel at ease. Get a friend to check whether anything other than your cue arm moves as you strike. If it does, make an effort to immobilise it. Get this right, and the stance you have is the right stance for you.

2. Your bridge is rock steady. Any movement of the bridge means movement of the cue, and you will not be hitting the cue ball where you aim — or where you think you are aiming. There are two ways of forming a bridge.

The first: place the hand flat on the table and spread the fingers as wide as is comfortable. Keeping them spread, raise the knuckles about two inches from the table and cock the thumb, making sure that the ball of the thumb is still resting on the table. With the lower half of the thumb resting against the knuckle of the first finger, there should be a V-shaped channel for the cue to run through.

The second: perhaps easier for someone still relatively fresh to the game. Tuck the third and fourth fingers of the bridge hand into the palm, then place the hand on the table with the thumb cocked. Keeping the hand in this position, unfold the two tucked fingers and the result is a perfect bridge.

3. Your bridge arm is straight, or as straight as is possible without beginning to feel uncomfortable. It would be silly to insist that your arm can be absolutely straight, but the most important thing is that you do not lean into the shot.

OK, I know that many players, including top ones, play with the arm bent. The reason I ask you to play with it straight is that when the pressure is on and you're 'under the cosh', you are likely to move your upper body and shoulder into the shot. With a straight arm, you can't move the other bits — it's impossible.

If you have this problem and decide to straighten your arm, you will probably find that your shoulder begins to ache. This is because you are stretching muscles that aren't used to it. Persevere. With practice this will soon pass.

It goes without saying, of course, that with difficult bridging and some cushion shots, the straight-arm approach is not possible.

4. Your grip is as if you have placed the cue on the table and picked it up as you would a hammer. You move down into the playing position with the same grasp on the butt. Remember, you are holding the cue, not gripping it, using only sufficient tension to stop it flying out of your hand as the shot is played. The cue is held with the thumb and first two fingers; the other two fingers only support the cue. There is no 'correct' place on the butt to hold the cue. This you will have to experiment with, because it depends on the balance of the cue, which should be of a length to enable you to hold it at the end, give or take a couple of inches.

5. Your cue arm, that is the upper arm, elbow and lower arm, are in a direct line with the cue. The elbow then acts as a hinge on which the lower arm swings back and forth like a pendulum.

On short shots, it is only the forearm that moves. With power shots, or those with lots of follow-through, the upper arm comes through after the contact is made with the cue ball. This type of action makes sure that the shot is not stunted or jerky.

Do not put your shoulder into the shot — ever. It may work for Alex Higgins and others, but this kind of sheer natural ability coupled with perfect timing is a rare combination. For most of us, a shoulder shot is a shoddy shot.

6. Your cue action is consistent and straight. Your cue is as horizontal to the table as you can keep it and you never 'seesaw'. You are delivering the cue absolutely straight at the centre of the white. You already know that any unintentional deviation off centre will impart unwanted side, leading to missed pots or poor position.

7. Your head keeps still. Movement of the head as the shot is played is probably the worst and most common fault of the players I watch. If the head moves, then the neck and upper body move and the cueing becomes inaccurate.

Take a simple example from another sport; shooting. Sighting down a snooker cue is much the same as sighting a rifle, except in our sport you're using both eyes. You wouldn't dream of aiming a rifle without your head being well down on the line of aim. Nor would you lift your head as you're about to fire. In shooting, you'd miss the target. In snooker, you miss the pocket.

8. Your eyes are flitting back and forth between three spots:
a) The cue ball and the point you intend the tip to hit.
b) The object ball and the point at which you want the white to make contact.
c) The pocket where, if everything goes right, the object ball will finish up.

Again, there are no rules about the order in which you should check these three points. Nor can anyone give you guidelines about how long you should focus on each. But the question most often asked is: where should I be looking when the shot is played? There is a definite answer to this one. At the moment of striking, the eyes must be trained on the object ball. Not the white, not the pocket, but on the object ball.

9. Your delivery of the cue is governed by lining up and aiming where you intend to hit the white. Obvious? Yes, but many players including professionals choose not to aim where they are going to strike. It works to their detriment. And many, many players don't have the ability to strike consistently where they aim.

You have picked your spot on the white and have addressed your tip to this point. Now comes the feathering, the back-and-forth movement of the cue before the actual shot. Hitting from a 'standing start' — that is, without feathering — makes for a hurried or jabbed shot.

Feathering is vital to ensure that we are continually aiming for the right spot on the cue ball and feeling for the right weight of shot to use. The feathering is not too fast. Make it easy and relaxed, like stroking a cat. The number of feathers varies from player to player. There is no right or wrong number — just be consistent.

Aiming complete, feathering finished, we're ready to pull back for the last time and propel the cue forward. To pause or not to pause? A long pause or a short pause at the end of the backswing? Experts disagree, but I believe in a slight pause for your brain to make last-minute adjustments to sighting and cueing. How quickly your grey matter can make these adjustments governs how long the pause is, so it is again a personal choice. But there should be a pause.

10. Your striking of the white is not a rushed movement. Your cue is accelerated smoothly from the full extent of the backswing to a point through and beyond the white.

How far to follow through? I don't think you need to worry about this particular argument, because if you keep the delivery smooth and unhurried, without jerking, the follow-through and the length of follow-through will be a natural part of your cueing.

Here are some points to run through after the shot if you feel your cueing is letting you down. Is the cue still pointing at the line of aim? Is the cue parallel to the bed of the table? Is your stance still in balance? Are your head and body in the same position at the end of the stroke as they were at the beginning?

If you can honestly tick off all ten points on this checklist, you can say you've scored the most important ten points of your snooker life. Make these ten points regularly, and you'll go on to make a lot more points on the table.

You are now ready for *Jimmy White's Snooker Masterclass.*

Charles Poole

1

The Nap Effect

Every decent snooker book tells you about the effects of the nap. Yet I still hear far too many players walk away from a perfectly good table that has a perfectly good cloth and say: 'Did you see that one roll off? Diabolical!' Sometimes this is an excuse for a bad shot, but most of the time it is the nap at work.

The nap of the cloth is made of millions of tiny fibres. These fibres always lie in one direction — from the baulk end up towards the top cushion. That is why a decently maintained table is always brushed and ironed in one direction — up the table.

I read a description once of the nap of the cloth being like the fur on a cat — stroke it in one direction and it feels silky smooth; stroke it in the other direction and you get nothing but resistance (and maybe even a couple of nasty scratches from the cat). Thinking of it this way might help you understand the effect.

Therefore, the fibres of the nap are acting like a barrier that is trying to stop balls played from the top of the table from going into baulk, and pull them towards the top cushion instead. Figure 1 shows how the nap works, with the lines slightly exaggerated to make the point.

It is worth remembering that every time you roll a ball on a snooker

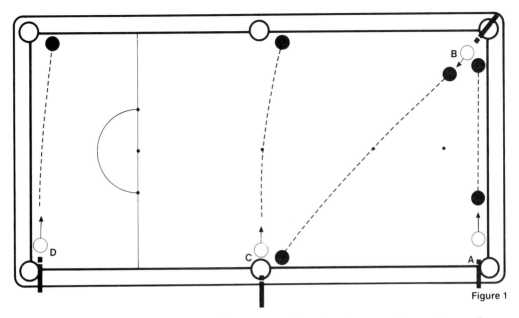

Figure 1

table, the nap will try to pull it towards the top cushion. Any other deviation means one of two things: either the table is not true, or you have played with unintentional side.

I should also say now that we are talking about the effect on slow-paced shots. With shots played harder, the pace of the ball is such that it cancels out the effect. The ball is not in contact with the cloth long enough for the nap to work on it. Figure 1 shows what happens with these slow-moving balls across the nap and angled against the nap. They are always trying to make their way towards the top cushion.

You probably already know that shot A is more of a certainty than shot D. Balls played along the baulk cushion will wander away from the pocket. A ball along the top cushion will hug it, and even come back on line if it bounces out slightly.

Shots B and C show that balls played across the nap tend to drift in the direction of the top of the table. You have to compensate for this by changing your aiming point — to the right-hand jaw of the pocket in shot B and the left-hand jaw in shot C.

When you watch professionals on championship tables, you will notice hardly any nap effect at all. This is because the cloth they use is super fine with very little nap. These cloths are not suitable for clubs, because they can't stand up to the wear and tear of constant use. Clubs usually go for thicker cloths with a heavier nap — hence more 'roll-off' and the more you need to allow for it.

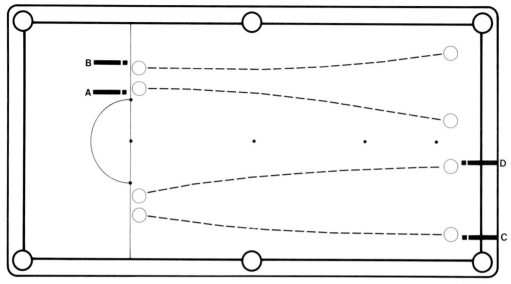

Figure 2

SIDE CAN CATCH YOU NAPPING

Place the white near the baulk line and play up the table, first with right-hand side and then with left. As you see in figure 2, and as is perfectly logical, the first will curl to the right and the second to the left. They obey the laws of reason. This is not so when you walk to the top cushion and play the same shots. Shot C, played with left-hand side, drifts right and shot D, with right-hand side, moves to the left.

I'm told that the scientific explanation for this was first published in a book around the turn of the century. But I haven't read it, and knowing whether it has to do with the first or the 21st law of physical motion will not make you a better player. What will matter to your game is that you remember and allow for the effect. When you apply side to slow-paced shots against the nap, the cue ball moves in the opposite direction to the side applied.

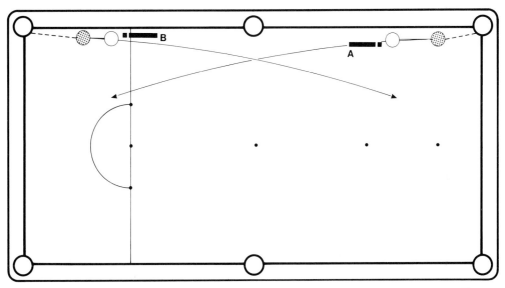

Figure 3

NAP AND THE SIDE-CUSHION SCREW

Faced with shot A in figure 3, with cue ball and object ball close to the side cushion, the average player will settle for making the pot. He will take his chances on the cue ball finishing close to the cushion for the next shot. The better player will be looking to screw back and away from the cushion after making the pot. This he will do by using bottom right-hand side.

When it comes to shot B, however, even better players can get themselves in a tangle. Logic tells them that to move the cue ball back and away from the cushion after the pot, they must apply bottom left. They try this, and are suitably baffled when the cue ball comes straight back along the cushion. It's our friend the nap up to its tricks again.

When a white is played with side against the nap, as in shot B, it will move in the opposite direction to the side applied. So in order to achieve the desired effect, you must forget logic and use bottom right-hand side to free the cue ball for the next shot. When playing this shot on the other side of the table, you must, of course, use bottom left-hand side — whether playing up or down the cushion.

To sum up, the rule for moving the white away from the cushion is as follows. When standing at the top end of the table and facing the baulk end, any screw-back cushion shots on the right-hand side of the table should be played with right-hand side; similar shots on the left-hand side of the table you play with left-hand side. It should be stressed that it's easier to remember the rule than it is to play this type of shot!

2

The Plain Truth about Off-centre Striking

Someone who had been at one of Terry Griffiths' excellent coaching sessions came back with some advice from the Welshman: unless you are regularly making 40 breaks, you shouldn't even be thinking about using side. That's good advice — but I'd go further than that. I would say that whether you're making 40, 80 or 100 breaks you should be avoiding side like the plague.

We all know the temptation. Put on bags of check and watch the crowd's reaction as the white comes clawing off the cushion at an unnatural angle. Or lay on the running side and wait for the gasps as the cue ball zips away at an incredibly wide angle. It's not necessary most of the time, honestly. Side may add to the spectacle, but it seriously affects potting and throw-off. You'll know that side pushes the white off path and influences the throw-off from the object ball. Why add to the complication and calculation?

Look at the simple example in figure 4. The object is to pot black and move the red from the side cushion. Use side and you have to get the pace right to compensate for the throw-off. Without side, using just bottom, the white will always travel straight. And without side, you are more likely to get the pot whether you hit hard or soft. The diagram shows varying

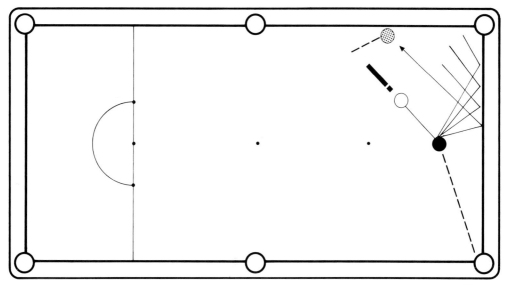

Figure 4

degrees of angle off the black, using just bottom and no side.

This is very straightforward. Using side gets tougher once the cue ball and object ball are farther apart. The greater the distance, the less easy the calculation, the greater the risk or misjudging. Why make it difficult? I just don't see the sense. In a situation where there is any chance to strike centrally below middle, always prefer this to side. Well, nearly always. There will be situations when it is in fact easier to play with a touch of side; but low central striking is a better shot most of the time. Why all this emphasis on plain centre or plain below-centre striking? The answer is that you have a better chance of staying in control of the forces that come into play every time you strike the white.

In figure 5, shot A is an example of extreme top. It's harder than it looks to strike high and in the exact middle of the white. (It's hard enough, let's face it, to strike dead centre of the white. The aim is to keep the cue parallel to the bed of the table, but in practical terms most of your shots are downward because you are cueing across cushions. It's surprising how many players misjudge where they're hitting the cue ball and are actually hitting above centre because they are looking down on the striking point.)

The moment your cue tip moves above centre of the white, you are applying downward pressure on the cloth and this leads to a squeeze effect between the ball and the slate. If you have not hit exactly middle, the cue ball will squeeze left or right, depending on which side your cueing has erred. The result is inaccurate striking of the object ball. In an extreme

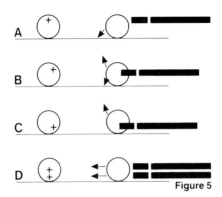

Figure 5

case, high-bridge and spider shots involving a downward cue action increase the pressure, which is why they are more difficult and less successful — unless the cue action is absolutely straight.

Shot B shows high, off-centre striking which produces not only the downward squeeze but a sideways push. As I explain elsewhere, you might mean this to happen and you make allowances in your aim. But often it happens by accident, and players stare in amazement as the pot stays out.

Thus, you can see the potentially disastrous effects of not one but two sets of pressure working against the cue ball. And working against you, too, if you did not mean to apply side in the first place.

Shot C shows how the downwards squeeze effect is eliminated if your stroke is off-centre but low. If you mean to play the white this way, there is an initial push-out effect early in the movement of the white. Thereafter, different things can happen depending on whether you're going with or against the nap of the cloth (see chapter 1). What we're working up to is the best possible argument for shot D: central or low-central striking. No squeeze, no push-out, and no mysterious forces are acting on the initial true direction of the cue ball.

I hope you're convinced about side. Its proper use gives your game a new dimension; its abuse or unintentional use will lead you down frustration alley. Be warned.

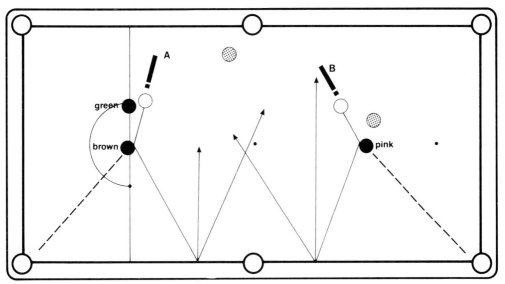

Figure 6

SIDE: IF YOU MUST, YOU MUST

Having said that you should avoid using side wherever you can because of the risks, I am going to state the obvious: there will be occasions when side is the only answer. We all face situations like those in figure 6.

Shot A: we are on brown and want to stay downtable for the loose red near the middle pocket. Plain-ball striking will give us a natural angle off the brown and cushion which will send the white away from the prime area. Check side, in this case right-hand side, is called for. The side holds the white off the cushion and on a line across the table rather than up the table.

Shot B: another situation where plain-ball striking will give us too wide an angle. After pink in the top, we want to stay uptable for the loose red. We could use lots of bottom without side to go charging down to baulk and back, but the necessary power makes it a difficult shot to control for cue ball placing. We would be bringing three cushions or more into play as well as risking an in-off. And it's very difficult to judge the pace of the white.

A check-ball pot, with left-hand side in this case, is the solution. White again holds off the cushion and, with the proper control, comes straight across the table for the red in the same pocket.

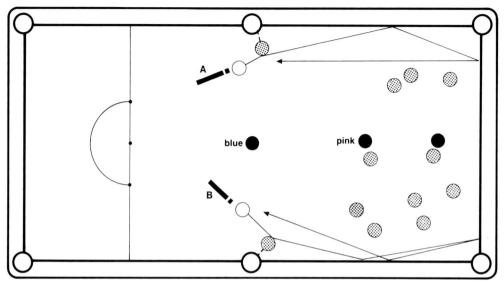

Figure 7

USING SIDE FOR POSITION

A very useful shot with side that you can build into your practice sessions is shown in figure 7. It helps with the control of side and judging the pace of the white when you are striking off-centre.

In shot A, pink and black are tied up, so you have to come down the table after the middle-pocket red. In this situation, plain-ball striking will guarantee no position because the white will career into the reds after coming off two cushions. A fair bit of left-hand side will narrow the angle off the top cushion and bring us more or less in a line down the table for blue or, if we over-run, one of the baulk colours.

Shot B shows a far more extreme use of side. The cut on the red is too fine to simply roll in and hold position on the blue. Therefore, maximum bottom right-hand side is called for. Playing bottom allows you to get more side on the cue ball. This is particularly useful when playing a thin ball, off which you can get little screw. The extra, anti-clockwise spring will bring white off side, top and side cushions again for downtable position.

With both these kinds of pots, side can be very useful; even when pink or black are not quite so cluttered with reds, and you need to hold position after a fine cut.

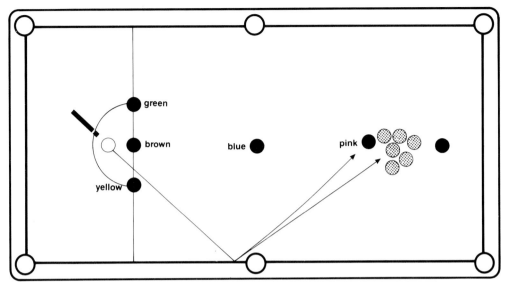

Figure 8

SOME MORE SIDE ISSUES

While we are talking about side, let's examine two more things: 'applied' side and side off the cushions.

Is it possible to transfer side from the cue ball to an object ball? It is one of those questions that seem to divide opinion among players. Many people say it is impossible, but I believe you can get an object ball spinning a little. Test it. Put the brown on its spot and the cue ball about a foot behind it in baulk. With extreme bottom side, strike the brown full face and hard. The colour, travelling up and down the centre spots, will come off path very slightly as it makes its second trip the length of the table.

The side you put on the white sets up a counter-side reaction on the object ball. If you play the white with bottom left, the brown comes off the top cushion slightly to the right, and vice versa with bottom right. But — and it's a big but — the effect is so marginal that it's practically pointless to bring it into your game. Over a distance of about 23 feet, you might get the object ball moving an inch off line. Even then, whether it does or not depends on cushions and the state of the cloth. For what it's worth, I say that you can impart side, although not enough to make much difference.

Side off the cushion is far more important. Look at figure 8 and you'll see a fairly common game situation. You are snookered behind the brown because your opponent has played a good safety shot with a cluster of reds still behind the pink. The escape is plain ball off the side cushion, right? It's amazing how many times I've seen a player go for this, only to trickle up and touch the pink, not the reds.

The explanation is that a plain ball, after hitting a cushion, always picks up side. This is because the cushion holds one side of the ball for an instant. The other side of the ball is free to move, and this sets up a slight rotation. In the case in point, the white picks up left-hand side — enough of it, as it travels up the nap, to make it drift to the left and miss the pack. The answer is either to play farther down the cushion, or if that's not possible, to compensate with a touch of right-hand side, which should cancel out the effect and keep the white on a truer path.

Also don't forget that the opposite is true when you're playing in the other direction — against the nap. A plain ball onto the left-hand cushion, for example, will pick up right-hand spin. If the white is travelling slowly, this spin acting against the nap will tend to make the ball drift to the left.

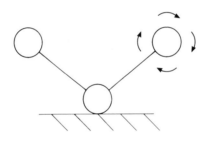

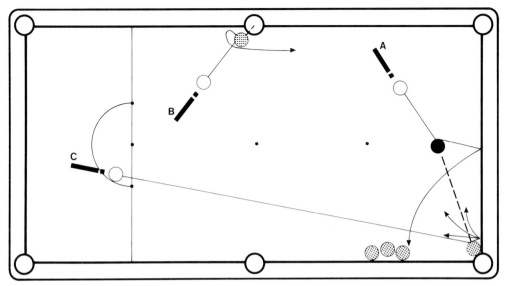

Figure 9

THE EFFECTS OF MAXIMUM TOP

Another aspect of off-centre striking is the matter of top, and in particular maximum top. The three shots in figure 9 show what maximum top can do, after the white has hit the object ball and then come into contact with a cushion. The extreme top going into the cushion becomes extreme bottom as it comes off, and when it is coupled with side can apparently alter the laws of nature.

Shot A is useful to move a bunch of reds grouped on the side cushion. Attach the black with extreme top right and the white will zing off the top cushion with a pronounced curve and give you a chance of disturbing the little pack.

Shot B is another useful one to know when going up the table for the black. If played plain middle ball, the natural angle would be to cannon the blue, so simply play it with plain maximum top.

Shot C enables you to leave the white ball in the top part of the table after taking a long red. Hit the white hard with plenty of top, although just plain top this time. As the cue ball comes off the top cushion, the top spin goes into reverse and the white will stop quickly. Depending on how thick or thin you contact the red, and with different degrees of top, you can keep the white in various areas of the top of the table. This is a handy shot when you are not sure if the table is true, because the pace of the white guarantees that you will eliminate any roll-off.

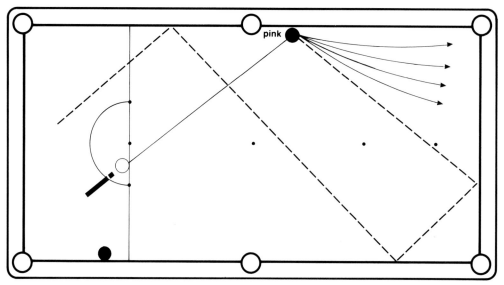

Figure 10

MAXIMUM TOP AS SAFETY

The effects of maximum top can also be a useful defensive weapon. Consider the situation in figure 10.

The pink is already safe, and you want to keep it that way. If you play it full-ball with top, the colour will run round the angles into baulk, whereas the cue ball will hold in the top quarter of the table. The application of different degrees of top and pace will enable you to dictate whether the cue ball slithers close to the side cushion or farther out.

3

Cushions: Friend or Foe?

Perhaps if Dennis Taylor had won the 1985 World Championship with his first attempt on the final black — a backwards double in the middle pocket — we would be seeing a different general attitude to the use of potting off the cushion. However, Dennis had to wait several shots more before he took the title with a straightforward pot on the final black — and the double remains a rare sight in top-class snooker.

You will no doubt have heard TV commentators say something like, 'He could play the double here, but I don't think we'll see him risk it'. Then you see the player try to screw a red down the side cushion at tremendous pace and we are all supposed to think that this is less dangerous than the double. I don't understand this thinking.

If players were to compare the percentage of doubles they can get with the amount of long pots they make, I think they would find that the double is far less chancy. A professional player can 'read' a table pretty quickly, and standards of tables are improving all the time. With all the skill that a top player has at his command, the double should not be a taboo shot. The good player should be able to make a successful double eight or nine times out of ten. I have watched some very moderate players who tend not to get punished for missed doubles because of the company

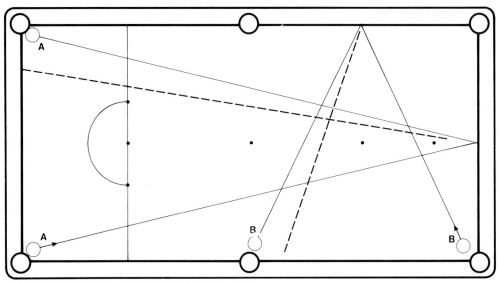

Figure 11

they play in. They play doubles at every opportunity and become pretty adept at them.

I suggest that you disregard this myth of the so-called risky double. This is not to say that you go for every double — but don't shy away from them either. Certainly, cushions vary and the rubber behaves differently from table to table, but a few pre-match minutes spent testing the trueness of balls coming off the cushion should arm you with enough confidence to go for the indirect pots when they arise.

Doubles are, of course, played by halving the angle between cue ball and pocket, and hitting the object ball at the point of the cushion which is exactly at that halfway point. The strength of the shot will make a difference to the angle of the bounce, though. As you can see in figure 11, if the ball comes into a cushion very hard, it tends to sink into the rubber rather than flick off it, and the result is a narrower throw-off. So if you are using any power on the shot, you will have to adjust your aiming point on the cushion to allow for this effect.

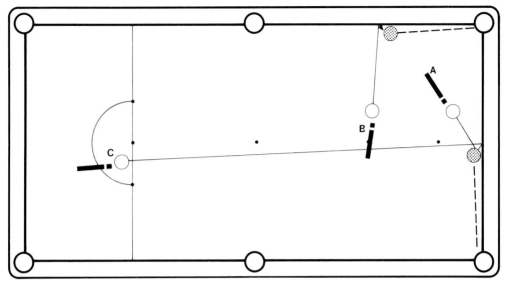

Figure 12

CUSHIONING THE POTS

Shot A in figure 12 is very easy if played without side. Just aim to hit cushion and ball at the same time. With practice, you'll find these hard to miss.

Shot B is a different proposition altogether. A stroke played with centre-ball striking on the white would have to be played very, very powerfully to get the object ball moving far enough along the cushion. In this case the white should be played with right-hand side and aimed cushion first. You are actually approaching the red from a thicker angle. If the object ball were on the opposite cushion you would need left-hand side on the white.

Shot C looks impossible. Can you really send the white ten feet to strike a ball on the top cushion and cut it in from a degree greater than a right-angle? You can. Maximum bottom right-hand side, cushion first, does the trick.

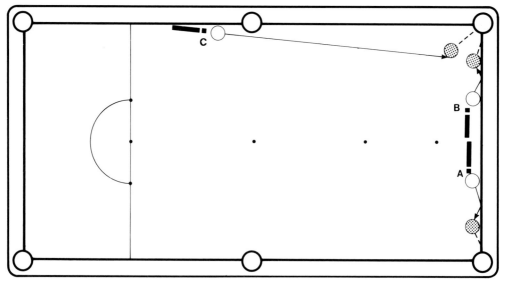

Figure 13

WHITE ON THE CUSHION

The white is on the cushion in the shots shown in figure 13. In both shots, even played plain ball, the white will pick up some spin because the cue ball is free to move on one side but held by the cushion on the other. You get unwanted side.

When the white and object ball are both touching the cushion as in shots A and B, never play the cue ball with side which is opposite the cushion. In other words, no right-hand side in shot A and no left-hand side in shot B. This 'opposite the cushion' side tends to throw the white into the cushion and off at an angle before it even comes into contact with the object ball. You miss what should be an easy pot.

The same principle applies to shot C, but because the object ball is away from the cushion, the pot is definitely on. Just remember to aim slightly thicker to compensate for the bit of unwanted right-hand side which the white will pick up as it comes away from the cushion.

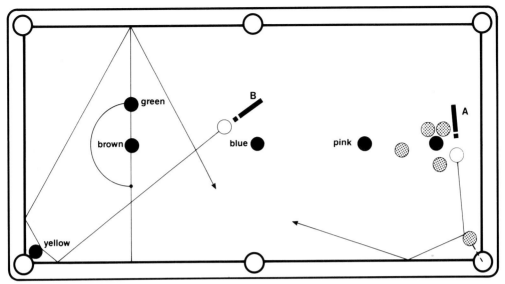

Figure 14

A STRAIGHT CASE FOR CUSHION FIRST

Playing cushion first to pot balls can be a very handy shot when you are left with a dead-straight pot.

In figure 14, shot A, there is a problem in going for the screw-back pot. Bringing the white back into the reds and black, and trusting to luck for positioning, could be a very short-sighted policy. Playing white cushion first, it is relatively simple to run down the table towards blue.

Shot B is a nice example. You are down to the colours and you are left a straight yellow hanging over the lip. It's tough to get on green unless you go cushion first and use the natural angle off bottom and side cushions for good position.

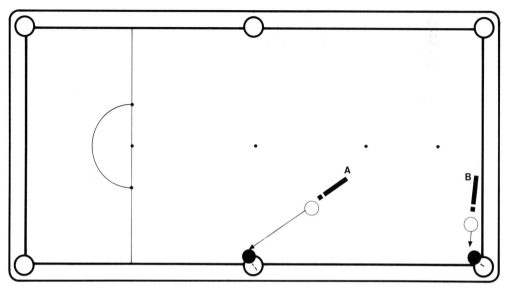

Figure 15

SQUEEZE, KISS, KISS

The two cushion shots in figure 15 can be handy, although I must confess that you might not get a chance to play them too often.

In shot A, the object ball is resting against the jaw of the middle pocket. It is impossible to cut in. Try the shot by playing right-hand side and hitting the object ball almost full-ball on the right. You get a squeeze and double-kiss result, which will make the pot.

The same applies in shot B, where the object ball is now resting against the jaw of the top pocket. Play it with bottom right-hand side and you can screw back a long way.

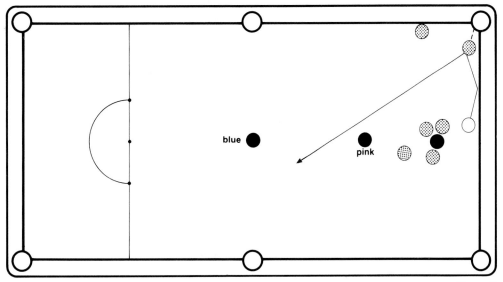

Figure 16

CUSHION-FIRST SCREW-BACK

This is not an easy combination shot at all, but one that can get you out of a difficult situation when the top of the table gets a bit crowded. Figure 16 shows how. Played simply cushion first, the white will cannon onto the red on the side cushion, leaving no position.

The secret is to play with screw — which is still on the cue ball as it makes contact with the red after the cushion — and the white will come back off the red and into the clear for a free colour. You will find it useful to experiment with varying degrees of screw, and screw with side.

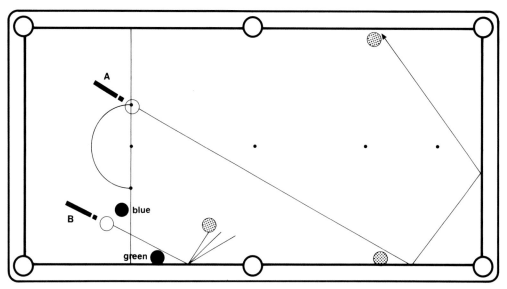

Figure 17

CUSHION SCREW

The cushions on a snooker table can be thought of as a wall. A very soft wall, certainly, but still an object off which we can bounce the white in different ways. You can even screw off the cushion.

Shot A in figure 17 is an example. The use of screw is a lot sharper than using side. Contact is made with the object ball in, perhaps, a snooker situation where no alternative direct solution is available. It is impossible to make the shot without deep screw. This is a useful exercise shot to show how much the screw off the cushion alters the angle. You can aim inside the first red and hit inside the second red.

Shot B, another snooker, can give us a really pronounced narrowing of the angle off the cushion if we use deep screw and make the cue ball really bite into the rubber.

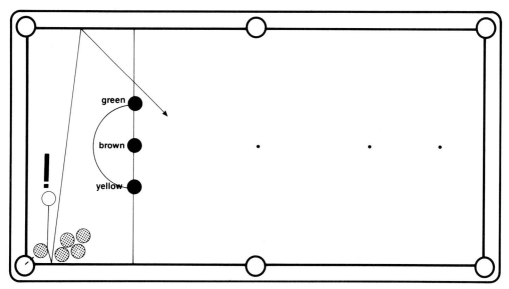

green

brown

yellow

Figure 18

CUSHION PLUS SCREW PLUS SIDE

Now we are getting really technical. Figure 18 illustrates the way that side can be transmitted from one cushion to another and used to your advantage. There's an easy red sitting begging over the bottom pocket, but there is no path through the traffic jam in baulk for either a plain-ball white or one played with right-hand side.

What we must do is pot the red as though we were playing a screwback with right-hand side; only we are using the cushion as the object ball. There will still be plenty of screw running on the cue ball as it contacts the cushion, because the red is struck thin. When the white runs across the baulk area and meets the opposite cushion, the side will bring it out nicely for a colour. A word of caution if you try this one: it works better on some tables and cushions than it does on others.

4

The Lure
of the Screw-back

Of all the shots in snooker, this is the one that gets people going. The novice yearns to play his first screw shot and will bash and crash and curse until he does. When he manages to get the white to come back six inches, he wants to do it like they do on the telly and amaze his friends with his ability to screw half the length of the table and more. Even experienced players and good amateurs overuse the shot and can't resist the temptation to draw gasps of admiration from the spectators by showing that their repertoire includes the deep, deep screw.

Sure, it's an attractive shot. It can be spectacular too. But, like any shot on the snooker table, it must be used for a purpose — and that purpose is not to amaze onlookers but to make position, keep scoring points and keep winning frames. Moreover, it is often a delicate shot rather than an extravagant one. Why screw back six feet when with an elegant soft screw of four inches you keep better position?

What is missing when most players get past the basics is the control of screw. It is worth spending a little time on this shot when you have some spare practice moments. Figure 19 is one way.

Put the blue on its spot and the white about six inches from it. Place five matchsticks on the cue ball side of the blue, starting with the first

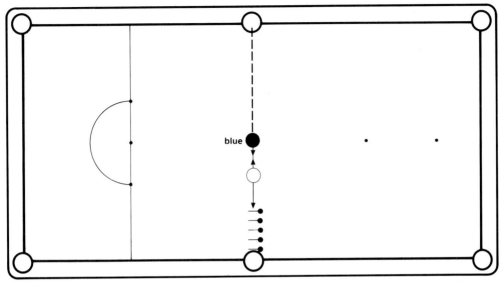

Figure 19

about two inches from the pocket and the others about an inch apart. Screw white off blue to touch the first matchstick — not to clout it, run over it or send it flying, just touch it. Once you have mastered this shot for weight, remove the first matchstick and repeat the shot on the second matchstick, and so on until you can pot the blue and screw to the last matchstick. It's a good exercise in controlling soft screw and will help you develop good touch. Here are some further tips on the screw-back shot.

Put plenty of chalk on the tip and lower your bridge by tilting the bridge hand. Stay down on the shot and be confident with the stroke — it is willpower, not raw power, that is required and you won't rip the cloth!

Aim low and hit low. I mean low. No, lower. Even lower! Most players are afraid to hit low and tend to pull out or up when they hit the cue ball. Remember to follow through.

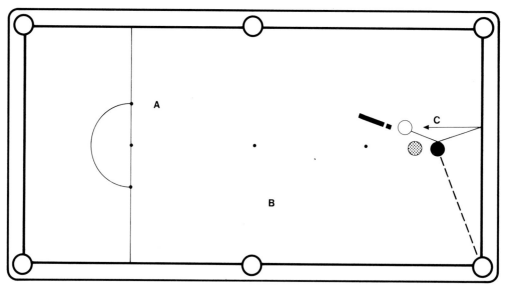

Figure 20

THE SCREW-CHECK SHOT

The problem in figure 20 is that you have potted the second-last red and landed on the black at quite a sharp angle. You want position on the last red but cannot roll in the black with the right strength to prevent the white coming off the top cushion and running down to the general area A. If you try the black by stunning off top and side cushions, you'll finish up around area B.

The way to play the shot is to screw the white into the top cushion with maximum bottom right-hand side, checking the cue ball into position C.

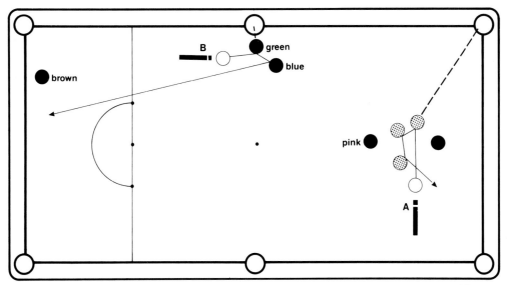

Figure 21

THE SCREW-BACK CANNON

Figure 21 shows two examples of this very useful shot.

In shot A there is a red on, but the gentlest of roll-in pots will still see the white running down the table and away from the high-scoring colours. The screw, coming back off the potted red, cannons onto the two loose reds and with any luck we find ourselves on the black. A bonus could be that the second cannoned red is moved away from the path which blocks the pink into the opposite top pocket.

Shot B is really a delayed screw-back. That's right — delayed. The cut on the green is so fine that the screw does not have time to bite until it comes into contact with the full face of the blue. White screws off blue, down the table for position on the brown.

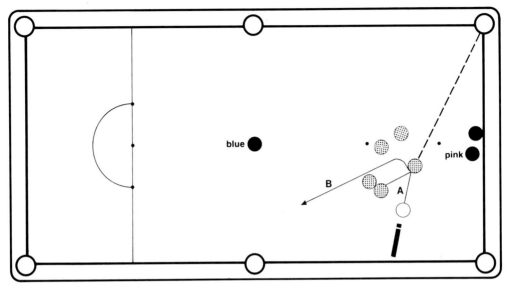

Figure 22

PUTTING SOME BOUNCE INTO THE SCREW

Ninety-nine times out of a hundred, players and spectators would say that screw involves hitting the ball low to produce backward or extreme throw-off movement of the cue ball. But they'd be wrong — or rather, not entirely right. You can also play screw without it being screw-back, at least at the start of the shot.

The shot is played with a downward strike on the white — but on the top part of the cue ball. A controlled power shot striking down in this way produces forward motion, but this is quickly followed by backward movement. Figure 22 shows the effect.

Pink and black are tied up and blue is the obvious colour after the loose red. But shot A, ordinary screw-back, would make the cue ball collide with the first of the pair of bunched reds and position would be lost. The answer is to play the bounce screw. The powerful strike downwards on the top of the cue ball will make the white bounce (it is no foul because you are not jumping over the object ball), and it will quickly convert its own forward movement into the round-the-corner shot B.

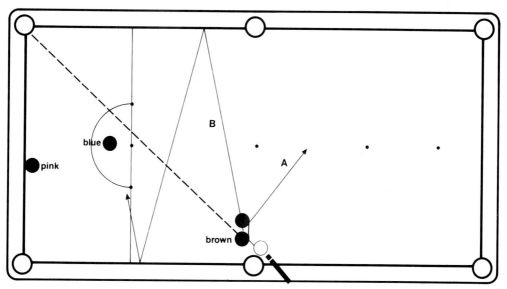

Figure 23

LEAPFROG — AND IT'S LEGAL

While we are considering the bounce screw, I might as well draw your attention to the only other kind of bounce shot that is legal in snooker. This is the bounce, or jump shot; used to gain position.

Figure 23 shows a pretty easy brown, but the prospect of position on blue looks hopeless. The natural angle for the white after hitting brown is marked A, but the position can be made by striking the top of white downwards hard. The white will leap over the intervening black and double off the far cushion to come across for blue.

Again, this is not a foul. The referee cannot pull you up for jumping over an object ball, because you have not done that. The object ball is brown, so it is perfectly legal to force the cue ball to hurdle the black.

5

Cannons Fire the Breaks

I suspect that you have often found that as the reds disappear one by one, the middle game disintegrates because the remaining reds are tied up against cushions, behind colours or in little, inaccessible clusters. This is where the pro's game is on a different level. Many top players have had experience with billiards and they use the knowledge they have gained from snooker's older brother to good effect.

The cannon is a most useful weapon to build into your snooker armoury. Shots which cannon a red away from the cushion, separate reds from colours or break up those little clusters can make the difference between being at the table for one stroke or several.

However, before we talk about different kinds of cannon shots, I would like to draw your attention to an important point about the pace of cannons. I can illustrate the point best by asking you to set up a little experiment on the table. Place the green and brown on their spots, and the cue ball on the yellow spot. You are going to try to cannon the brown off the green and into the green baulk pocket.

Play the brown hard and you will find that it strikes to the left of the pocket opening; play it softer and you will make the pot. The reason is that with the first shot, the hard cannon, the brown hits green before it

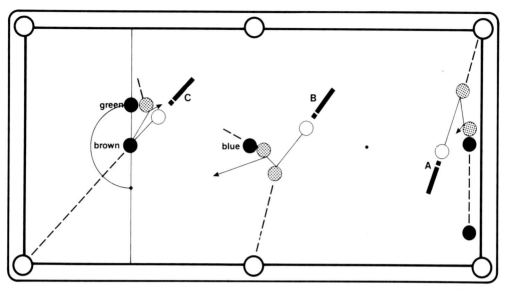

Figure 24

has begun to rotate at all. In effect, it is skidding across the cloth with the same effect as if you had played the brown as the cue ball with stun. The speed of the shot has to be taken into account, and the true cannon effect — without the unwanted stun — will follow with a medium-paced shot that gives the brown time to begin rolling.

I shall use several labels for the different kinds of cannons we will examine, but it doesn't matter whether you call them positional cannons, multi-purpose cannons, holding cannons or whatever. The important thing for your game is that you keep an eye open for them — and go for them, as long as they don't hinder the pots.

MULTI-PURPOSE CANNONS

Let's start with what you might call multi-purpose cannons, as in figure 24.

Shot A is a screw-back plant cannon. The black is tied up on the top cushion almost against a red. The right shot is to take the opportunity of disturbing those two balls while making the first red. We do this by screwing back to knock the awkward red onto the black, pushing the black towards the opposite corner pocket. Executed properly, this plant cannon can leave a more accessible black to pot — and the chance that the disturbed red has come out a little, into a better potting position. That's a pretty good example of the multi-purpose cannon.

Shot B is similar, except that the half-ball cannon is aimed at sending white a little downtable off the second red. With some luck the cannoned red should push the blue into a pottable middle-pocket position, thus freeing itself for potting after the blue goes.

Shot C is a simple one. The last red is tucked up against the green, and a straightforward soft screw from the brown will clip the red clear for potting in the green pocket.

All three shots are good examples of how important it is to plan ahead as you build a break. Usually, none of them would offer themselves to you on a plate. You have to look for them and get in a position to play them. This in turn means that you should be thinking about getting into position for the cannon when you play the previous shot. Difficult? Of course it is, but being good at something is never easy!

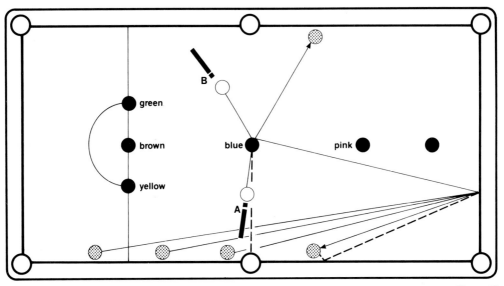

Figure 25

SIDE-CUSHION CANNON

During just about any reasonably-sized break, you will eventually come across the problem of a red sitting on a side cushion.

If the red is above the pink spot and you have any choice in the matter, as in figure 25, try for position B rather than A on the blue. The run-through cannon off shot A is a pretty difficult one to make. Your initial position on the blue would have to be spot-on.

However, shot B, with the white slightly more baulkside of blue, will allow you to play off the top cushion and come down to disturb the red.

Here a slight miscalculation will not be a problem, because you'll still make the cannon if you hit cushion-first. The red will still be clipped out more into the open. Different degrees of side will allow you to move a red from varying places along the side cushion, as shown in the diagram.

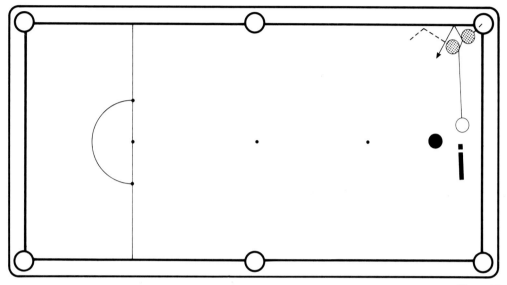

Figure 26

THE HOLDING CANNON

Figure 26 shows an easy pot of the farthest red. The problem is that if we play the red over the pocket first, the cue ball is likely to come off the side cushion, clip the second red and finish close to the top cushion — and out of position.

A cannon played with left-hand side moves the first red, pots the second and clears a path for the white to come out for a straightforward pot on the black.

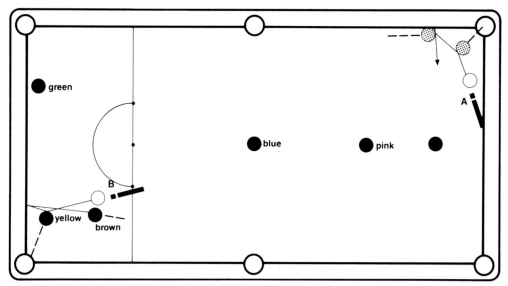

Figure 27

MORE HOLDING CANNONS

The cannon can also be a great help in taking the speed off the cue ball, particularly when the white snicks a fine cut and threatens to run too far away from preferred position. The two examples in figure 27 illustrate the holding or positional cannon.

In shot A, the fine cut is the obvious ball. By kissing full-ball into the red on the cushion, we can hold the cue ball for position on the black. There is also a chance that the cushioned red will be pushed into better position. Either way, we're on black rather than careering down the table.

The same principle is at work in shot B. We play the fine cut on the yellow but do not want to run too far away from the green. The cannon off the baulk cushion to kiss the brown full-ball will hold the white in baulk.

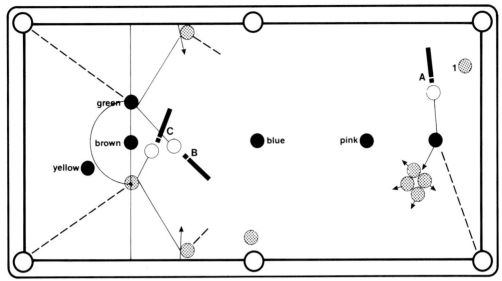

Figure 28

THE CANNON 'FOR LATER'

The cannon is not only a useful shot for keeping a break going — it can also be played to move balls for a later stage in a break. You might call these tactical cannons.

In figure 28, shot A offers a simple roll-in on the black, leaving position on red 1. But wait. You would have to get reasonable position on red 1 to set yourself up for perfect position on the second black, in order to split the cluster of reds. It is far better to open the mini-pack now — while you have the chance — without running the risk of getting out of position. Run the white through after potting the first black and split the group. Even if they fall unkindly for you, you still have red 1 to fall back on, then black and possibly a second chance to disturb the bunched reds if they have not opened up favourably.

Shot B shows another position where we should go for the tactical cannon, knowing that all is not lost if it fails. Potting green, with enough force to cannon onto the side-cushion red, still leaves us the option of a loose red over the opposite pocket if the cannon doesn't come off. If it works, we might be able to pot the cannoned red next, and leave the other red over the middle pocket as an insurance.

Shot C is a little riskier, because we're aiming to pot one red, cannon a second red into the open and stay on a colour. But the risk is worth taking, because from this position we'd be very unlucky indeed not to find ourselves on a colour after the cannon.

These three examples reinforce the message, I hope, that the player who can think ahead like this whenever the chances arise, is far more likely to build up points and breaks. That is one of the secrets of being a good player.

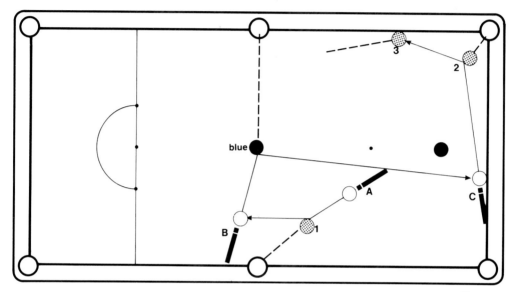

Figure 29

LOOKING FOR THE CANNON ANGLE

Another example of how the thinking player will be looking for the chance to shift an awkward red on the cushion can be found in figure 29. We want to keep the break going, and the only way to do this is to think a couple of steps ahead.

A pot on red 2 from position A would give us an easy black to follow. But the pot is too straight to cannon the white onto that troublesome red 3 on the side cushion.

A better choice is red 1, running through a little below the blue. We've got to get on red 2 in such a way as to be able to pot it and move red 3. A thick stun on the blue brings the white up to the top cushion, and now we have created the angle to pot red 2 and bring out red 3. The cannon will hopefully move the last red out towards a pottable middle-pocket position and we are still on pink or black.

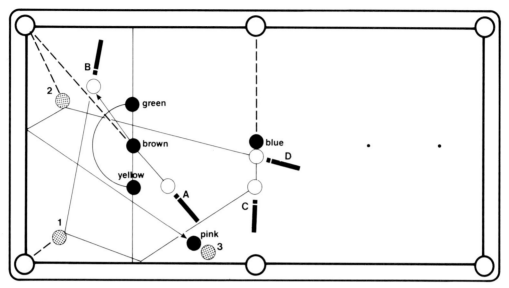

Figure 30

CANNONS: IF AT FIRST YOU DON'T SUCCEED ...

Here is a little sequence in figure 30 that shows how the good player, even though he doesn't make every shot he goes for, might work up to a successful cannon.

We have just taken the fourth-from-last red and we have our eye on the red which is tucked up behind the pink and unpottable. This must be cannoned out at some stage, if the break is not to collapse quite soon.

Shot A is a run-through pot on brown. We are looking to leave ourselves an angle off red 1 to move red 3. The screw pot off the side cushion misses the cannon we were looking for, but we're on blue anyway. We still have to look for an angle off the next red, 2, to give us the elusive cannon.

A stun pot on blue leaves a cut on red 2 but not so fine that we can't bite into the red and stun off the baulk cushion. This time we hit the pink onto the hidden red and, if we get the run of the ball, we'll find that red 3 is in the open and available.

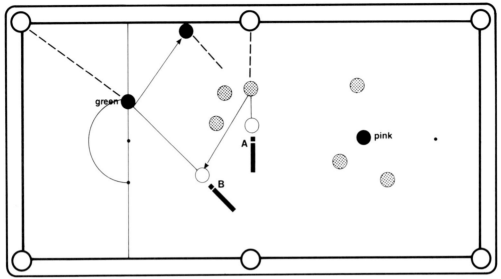

Figure 31

CANNONS: WHEN TO HOLD YOUR FIRE

I've advised you to be on the lookout for cannons; but at the same time, don't go scouring the table for them and diving headlong into them as soon as you see them. Sometimes it is possible to shoot for your cannon too soon, or go for one when it is technically better to avoid it.

Figure 31 is a case in point. An easy red in the middle gives you a chance to move the black with a cannon. But if you overhit slightly and the white catches the far side of the black, you'll find yourself with the black out and the white stuck below the baulkline.

Alternatively, screw off the red for green and with this pot you can look for your cannon on the black. If you catch the toptable side of the black and run up the table, there are reds up there which might save the day. You want to catch the black full face and stay where the loose reds are available for the centre pocket. Even if you hit black on the baulk side, the cue ball will remain in the right area.

Sometimes it will not be to your advantage to move a cushioned ball, such as black in this situation. If you have a good lead, it would be better to take three reds with baulk colours and keep the black tied up.

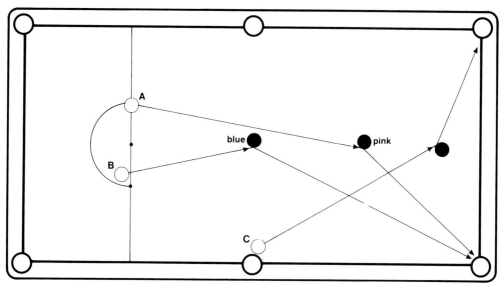

Figure 32

CANNONS GALORE: THE IN-OFF VERSION

I mentioned earlier that many good snooker players have felt the benefit of having played billiards. One of the core skills of billiards, the half-ball in-off, can play quite a role in the break-making of the snooker player who wants to advance his game. At first glance, the shots in figure 32 look like billiards shots. Well ... they are after a fashion, but they have real applications in snooker, and they should be practised and the angles memorised.

All three shots here are played half-ball without side. (In shot A it is far easier to go in-off pink than it is to pot.)

You can use this knowledge of the half-ball angle to pot a red over a pocket if there is no clear path to it for the white. The instinct of many players is to use one red to pot another when the direct-pot path to the pocket is blocked. But you will find that it is ten times easier to cannon the cue ball off the first red to pot the second.

Take a few minutes to practise these in-off shots, from both sides of the table, and become familiar with the throw-off of the cue ball. The knowledge will come in very handy — particularly over the next few pages!

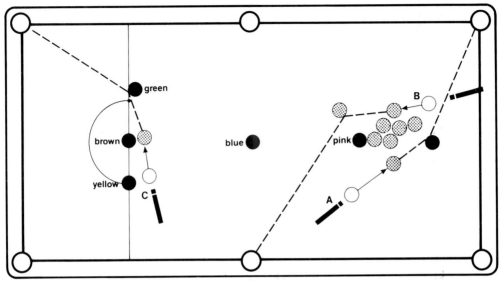

Figure 33

CANNONS THAT ARE WORTH A TRY

I'm sure I will be accused of getting into the realms of fantasy or trick shots when I talk about the possibility of the in-off cannon. That is, striking the white to hit an object ball onto a third or fourth ball for the pot. Some people will say they are too risky. However, risk is governed only by skill, and what would be risky to the club player would be a good chance to a professional. Look at the three examples in figure 33. I think you'll agree that the degree of chance-taking is not that great.

Shot A has a loose red that will not pot directly into the top pocket. A cannon pot off the black will work, but if it misses you'll be safely hiding behind the pack.

Shot B could be even more useful, cannoning the loose red from the edge of the pack, off the second red into the middle. A little screw-back leaves you on black if it goes in, and pretty safe if it doesn't.

Shot C can be a real match-winner if it happens to be the last red. Stunning the white behind brown, you attempt to pot the red off the green into the bottom. If it goes, you are on brown. If it doesn't, and even if it sits over the hole, your opponent is snookered.

Even if you do decide that these shots are too danger-prone for matchplay, you can use them in practice matches to keep a break going when there is no other shot on.

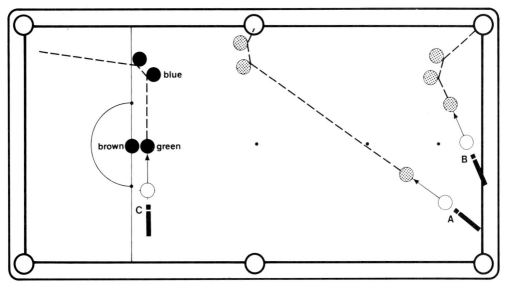

Figure 34

ONE, TWO, THREE — BUT NOT EASY

Let's be honest — the kinds of cannons shown in figure 34 are far from easy to make. Most players would probably say they are too difficult or chancy even to try. However, the talented amateur or the professional would think them worth a go if the game situation warranted the inherent risk. Again, higher skill equals lower risk.

Shots A and B are cannons off two balls, used when the first red has no clear route to the pocket. Shot C is the kind which should be within the reach of most people, because we are not looking for the pot. Stun the white, take the green off the other two balls towards the baulk cushion and your opponent is snookered.

6

Pots Out of Nowhere

I'll bet that you have often seen a top-class player make a pot and said to yourself, 'I didn't think he had enough room to squeeze that one in'. It happens. If you look very closely during your next match or practice, and you know what you are looking for, you might pick up some shots which at first glance you would dismiss as impossible.

Figure 35 shows two such examples. In shot A, the red appears to interfere with an otherwise straightforward pot of the blue into the middle pocket. There does not seem to be a way to pot the blue without striking the red first, and a plain-ball stroke will see the blue following a natural angle to miss the pocket.

You can make this shot by using extreme bottom right-hand side. This has the effect of narrowing the natural angle of the object ball.

Shot B is similar, but this is for position rather than the pot. The open red is a fraction off straight. A plain-ball pot will cannon the cue ball into the pink, but our objective is to run through for the black. Played with left-hand side, the white will go through straight and throw the object ball into the pocket.

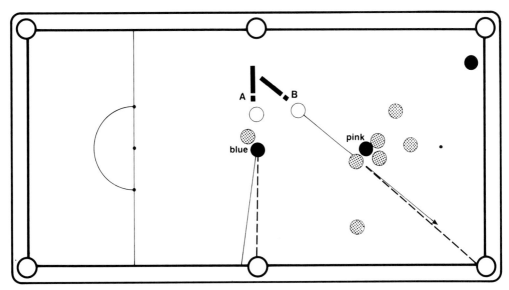

Figure 35

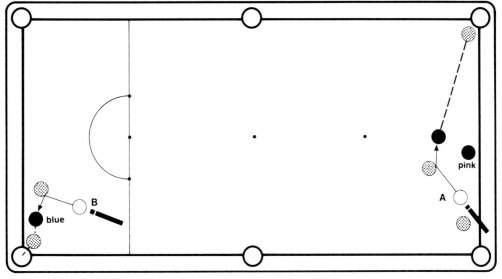

Figure 36

PLANTING IDEAS

The cannon plants in figure 36 can turn a blind alley — an easy red with
no colour available — into a break-making opportunity.

In shot A, you are too far behind on the scoreboard to be able to think
of potting anything but high-value colours. Here you can cannon off the

red onto the black, which in turn cannons the easy red into the pocket. It is highly unlikely that the black will have enough pace to drop into the pocket itself because much of its momentum will be transferred to the red. The shot should leave an easy black near the pocket for the break to continue.

Shot B is easier because the balls are closer, but the same principle applies. Cannon the white off the first red onto blue, to pot the easy red and leave an equally easy blue in the same pocket. A bonus is that the first red will come out into a more open position.

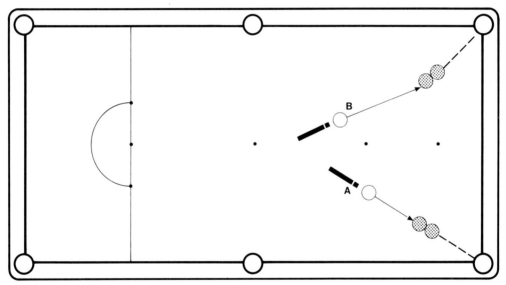

Figure 37

PUTTING ON THE SQUEEZE

Shot A in figure 37 is one that will be familiar to most players, and is an elementary shot to make. The reds are touching and in a line with the pocket. Any fairly full contact on the first red will pot the second.

Shot B is a different proposition. The reds are touching, but in a line to miss the pocket by about two inches. Clearly, we could make a pot by hitting the first red on the side to throw the second red onto a path for the pocket — but which side? The answer is the 'wrong' side. Or, at least, the side opposite the one that looks the most logical. In this case, it is contact not on the left-hand side of the red, but on the right.

The effect has something to do with the squeeze effect, as the force is transferred between the touching balls. I don't understand the science of it, and I'm not sure if anyone else does either. Still, the fact remains that it works, and can be a most valuable piece of knowledge early in a game, when the pack is disturbed but the reds are still fairly close. Watch out for this one. Play the opposite of what common sense tells you, and you will make the pot.

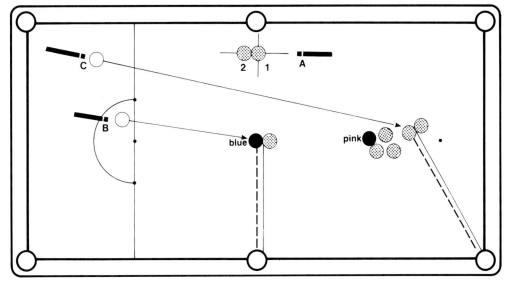

Figure 38

THE RIGHT ANGLE FOR A PLANT

Being able to spot the 'hidden' pots will add to your break-making ability. The illustrations in figure 38 give another kind of example.

Shot A is simplicity itself to make. A line drawn through the centres of the two reds would be at right angles to a line drawn through the centre of the first red to the pocket. The first red will pot as long as the cue ball strikes it thinnish on its left-hand side.

To test this, place the blue on its spot, as in shot B, and put a red directly behind it and touching it. From the D, strike the blue thinnish on its left-hand side. You've got the pot.

How often does this situation arise in play? More often than you might think. Admittedly, not always in as obvious a situation as in shot B, but often there is this kind of shot hiding away in the pack of reds. Take shot C as an example. Look for it, go for it and there's a good chance that you'll not only pot the red but open up some more for a break-making opportunity.

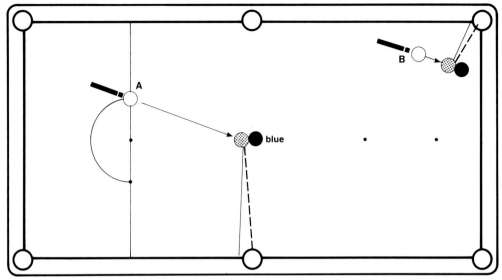

Figure 39

SQUEEZE, JOSTLE AND POT

You can help create a potting angle by the way you approach balls which are touching or almost touching. Two more examples of 'pots out of nowhere' are shown in figure 39.

In shot A, the red will not go if it is struck finely. It will follow the natural angle and strike the cushion below the middle pocket. Hit this kind of ball thick, bearing in mind that you are trying to keep the red and cue ball in contact with each other for as long as possible. You are setting up a squeeze and jostle effect which will move the blue away and enable the red to find and follow a wider angle towards the pocket.

Shot B is similar, but near a top pocket. The natural angle for the red is to come off black and strike the side cushion. Hit thick, it stays in contact with the white for a split second longer and will throw off on a wider angle to make the pot.

COMBINATION PLANTS

What we have been saying so far about touching ball plants, right-angle plants and in-off cannons can sometimes be used in combination. Look at the next three diagrams (figures 40, 41 and 42) and see if you would have spotted these 'unpottable' balls.

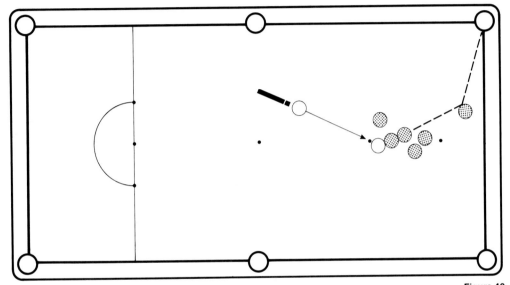

Figure 40

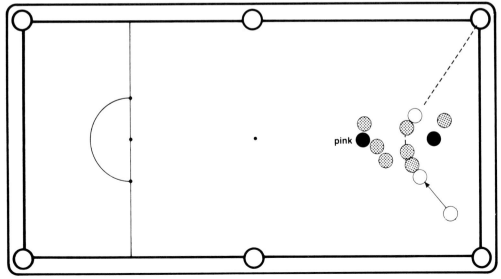

Figure 41

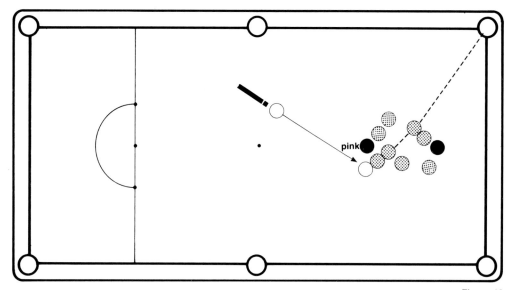

Figure 42

7

Building Your Break-making 'Luck'

Snooker's a funny game. It's nearly always the other guy who gets the run of the ball. The ones who beat you always seem to have good fortune in what's left on the table, and seem to have three reds to choose from, when you're lucky if you get one!

It seems even more unfair that the professionals break down far less frequently than everyone else. They make an opening break of 20 or 30, reach the point where lesser mortals run out of choices or steam, or both — and yet still have balls lying just right to make a 50 or 60 break.

Take a closer look. Watch how the outstanding break-makers at the highest level are continually manipulating balls around the pink and black spots. Forget luck — see how they often ignore the 'easy' pot to enable them to bring off the little pushes, nudges and cannons that promote balls into pottable positions.

Keeping your options open, sometimes shunning the easy red, taking out insurance against things going wrong and thinking ahead are all at the very heart of successful break-making. Over the next few pages we will look at these techniques and ideas. Think about them. Practise them. Build them into your game, and you'll probably find that your 'luck' suddenly improves!

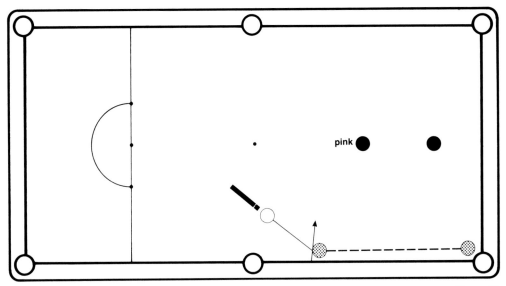

Figure 43

Take as an example the situation in figure 43. There is a red begging to be sunk in the top pocket and the reaction of most unknowing players is predictable, 'Great — an easy red for a change. The only problem is staying on the black'. Wrong. The better player will be asking himself how *not* to pot that red. He will want to save it in case he fails to get position on another red or, as in this case, to move an awkward red into a position that helps him continue the break.

The better player here will roll the awkward red up the cushion to sink the easy red, so that it replaces the first red. A difficult red has been turned into a sitter, and the break can continue after the colour.

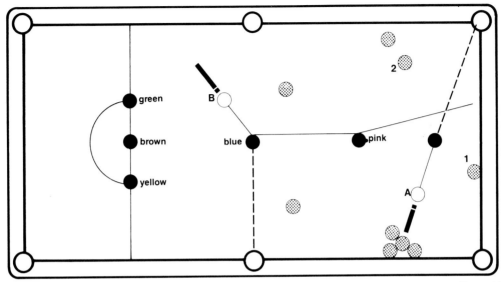

Figure 44

THE 'INSURANCE' BALL

It pays to take out insurance against things going wrong in a break. Since most really big breaks contain an element of good fortune, it is logical that they will also hold some misfortune — and the good player plans for this.

We know that the nap is going to pull a slow or medium-paced ball towards the top cushion when it is played across the table. This means that a loose red which can be taken along the top cushion is almost a certainty — and we must not waste it. As a break is built, this kind of red must be saved for an emergency — an 'insurance' ball, if you like.

Shot A in figure 44 shows how valuable it can be. We have just potted another red and finished too straight on the black. To play with top invites the in-off, and if we try the screw-back and cannon into the four grouped reds we are trusting to luck about how we are going to finish. The way the reds are placed here, it is hard to get enough pace on the screw to really break the reds free. The insurance ball, red 1 on the top cushion, is the saviour. Had we potted this one earlier in the break, we would have been facing bigger problems now.

Shot B shows another argument for insurance. The angle onto the blue forces us to look for a cannon on the pink, with the idea of dropping into position on red 2. The pink was clipped too finely and the white has run through onto the top cushion. Enter the insurance red. There are many ways that you can finish on the top cushion — and isn't it a good job that you're a handy player and have left a red there, just in case?

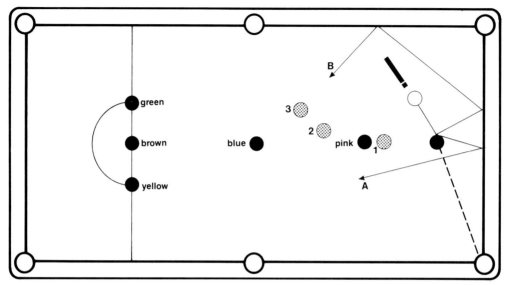

Figure 45

OPENING UP THE OPTIONS

TV commentators, trying to help the viewing audience 'read' a break as it develops, are often heard to make the either-or statement, 'Now he can either stun this red for the pink in the middle or run through on the right side of the blue'. How is it that the Davises, Whites and Knowleses of this world can have so many options? The answer is that we create the choices by planning for *not* getting on the next red. In other words, we play positional shots which give us an escape route if we miscalculate — which we all do from time to time!

Look at figure 45. We are on black and have a choice. We can run through to leave the white around position A, to take red 1 into the opposite top pocket. If the cue ball does not travel far enough — and half an ounce of strength too little will do that — we will be facing a cut on the red which makes the next position much harder.

The alternative is much more satisfactory. Stunning the white off top and side cushions into position B, we can continue the break quite happily, even if we are not inch-perfect. As we walk round to play the shot, we can choose to roll red 1 into the top or, if we have overstruck, still have the choice of reds 2 or 3 in the middle. The permutations in this kind of positional play are endless. The lesson is, I think, clear: play the shot that gives you the greatest number of options for the next shot.

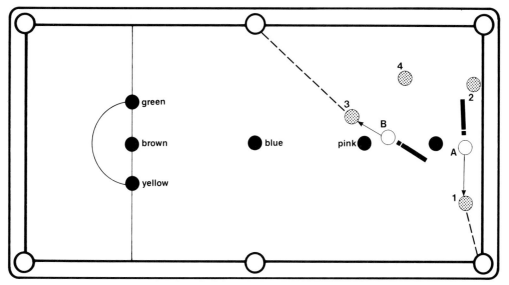

Figure 46

AVENUES OF SUCCESS

No amount of good potting will keep a break going if balls are blocking the paths of the colours to the pockets. It makes sense therefore, when you are faced with a choice of reds, to make a beeline for the ones which clutter the avenues for the high-value balls.

Take shot A in figure 46, for example. You have a choice of two reds. Red 1 is favoured because it frees the black into both top pockets for later in the break.

Shot B shows a similar choice, with reds 3 and 4. It is wiser not to be tempted by red 4 at this stage. By taking red 3 in the middle, you will free the pink and make it pottable in any of the six pockets should you need it.

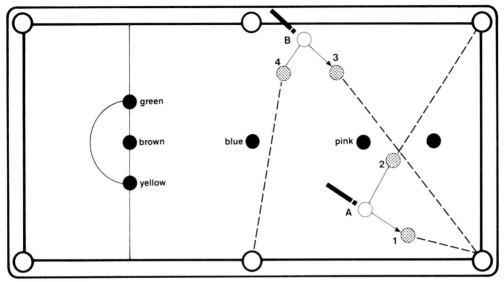

Figure 47

WHICH RED?

Your break-making will become more fluent, and break down less often, if you can try to keep loose reds towards the middle of the table. One of the secrets of building these big scores is to leave yourself reds which are pottable in more than one pocket. The trick is to take the 'single option' red first, when the chance arises. Figure 47 shows two positions where you have such a choice of reds.

In shot A, it makes sense to go for red 1 now, while you have a good angle, because you might have to work hard to find the red as available later in the break. Red 2 can be potted into either of the top pockets and at least one of the middle pockets, so save this one.

A similar approach should be taken when you are faced with the choice shown in shot B. Each red is as difficult as the other. Nevertheless, you are unlikely to get an early chance to take red 3 as simply as you can now, so that's the one to go for. Furthermore, by taking red 3, you are leaving red 4 out in the open for a pot in the middle. The principle for selecting the red is, therefore, go for the one which is going to leave the other reds in the middle of the table.

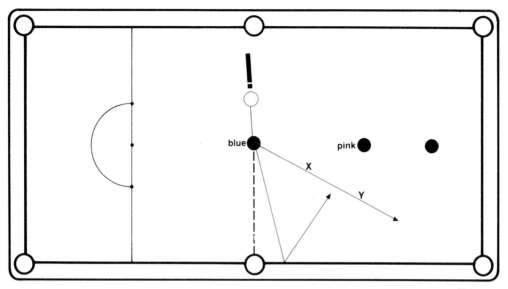

Figure 48

RUN THROUGH WITH LESS RISK

Part of the art of break-making is to limit the chances of a shot going wrong. Figure 48 shows an example. A simple run through, rather than the alternative stun or screw shot, gives you a much better chance to stay on your next ball.

The stun shot from the blue will put you on pink, but only between the points marked X and Y on the cue ball's path. You would have to be pretty near perfect with your placing to be able to take pink and then black.

In this case, it is much better to roll the white through, off the side cushion. Coming off the cushion, the white is on a line to give you position on the pink, with a far greater allowance for getting the pace wrong.

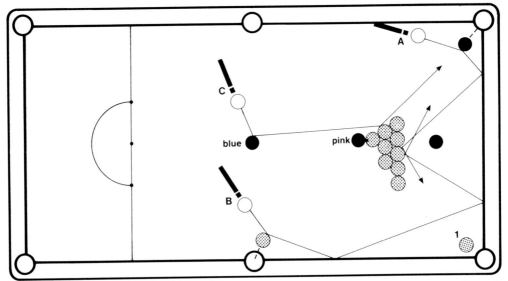

Figure 49

THE TRIANGULAR 'WALL'

Many players will avoid striking the triangle of reds early in a frame unless they are trying to split them open. However, you can think of the group of reds as a triangle-shaped wall, off which you can bounce the white into position. The added benefit, as you gain this position, is that the cue ball can jostle reds out of the cluster for later in the break.

I'm not trying to kid you. You may find some merit in the kinds of shot displayed in figure 49, which give you position off the pack. Shots A and B are quite risky, but worth trying if your cue arm is working well and your confidence is up.

Both shots A and B are from positions where the thinness of the cut makes it just as hard to get on another colour as it is to play for position off the pack. When they come off perfectly, you're nicely on the black, hopefully, with some freed reds.

Shot C is slightly different. Here, you are trying to pot blue and dislodge reds as you make position on red 1 over the top pocket.

The good aspect of these shots is that you are jostling the pack for an easy red. Even if you come out with no shot on, you can play safe. By comparison, when splitting the reds from a spotted colour (the standard ones are black or blue), the pot is harder, has to be hit firmly and leaves the reds open for your opponent if you miss.

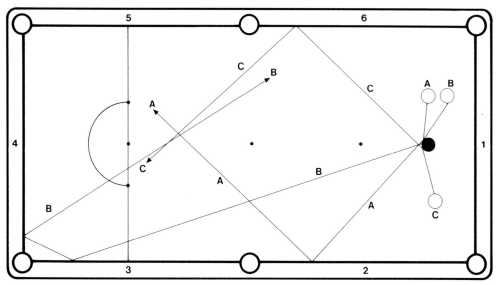

Figure 50

THE LAST RED: THINK YELLOW

The frame is down to the last red, and you are in a position to take it and drop onto black. Stop. Don't become mesmerised by the second shot in this sequence — the seven-point ball — but concentrate your planning on the yellow.

If you don't want the break to falter, you have to give serious thought to where the white must lie in relation to the black, so that you can get down for the yellow after that. In figure 50, I have numbered the cushions to help the explanation.

Shot A, just off straight to the black, is one that is often left. Follow the path of the cue ball off cushion 2 and you will see that there is little margin for error in the pace. Hit the white too soft and you'll need the rest. Hit it too hard and you leave yourself with a fine cut on the yellow, and every extra roll of the white towards cushion 5 increases the difficulty of taking the yellow and staying on green.

Shot B, with the cue ball nearer cushion 1, is easier — even though a stun shot off cushions 3 and 4 is called for. You have far fewer problems with the pace of the cue ball, because once it passes the baulk line on its way up the table, it can still travel as much as six feet before the yellow becomes a difficult shot.

Shot C is ideal if you can manage to get the white here after the last red. It gives you a straightforward roll-in on the black, with a natural line down to the yellow off cushion 6. Again, even if you misjudge the speed of the cue ball, you have a fair margin of error as the white runs down towards the D.

As a general rule — unless you need black, pink or blue — it is easier to go for a baulk colour after the last red. That way you stand a better chance of getting the desired position on yellow.

8

Safety and Snookers

You don't win matches by going for every 50-50 pot on the table, and many times discretion is the better part of valour — and a match-winner too. The following pages deal with general approaches to safety play, and the supreme safety shot — the snooker.

My first suggestion is that you should not be ruled by convention. Be on the lookout for different ways of making things really tough for your opponent, rather than the 'standard' way. It seems to be branded on the brains of snooker players at all levels that a safety shot must consist of the cue ball being tight on the bottom cushion and the object ball on the top cushion. Some of the risky shots that are played to make this happen make the words 'safety play' laughable. Figure 51 shows a couple of examples of situations where you should get rid of this 'standard' approach and try to make things unpredictably difficult for your opponent.

Shot A could be played by sending blue into baulk and white up the table. You can be equally sneaky — and do it a lot more simply — by glancing a shot off the blue to leave a snooker behind any one of the baulk colours.

Shot B depicts a position where all your indoctrination suggests that

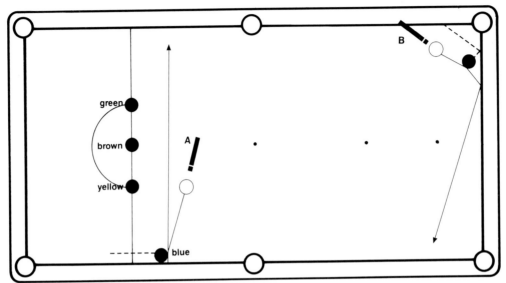

Figure 51

you clip the black thinly to leave the balls at opposite ends of the table. If you're going to be nasty, do it with relish. Play it as shown, and you will have left your opponent a much harder reply safety.

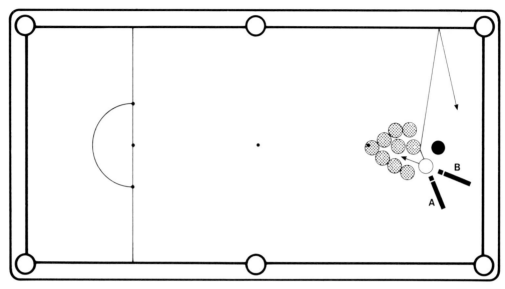

Figure 52

DO UNTO OTHERS BEFORE THEY
DO UNTO YOU

Another safety shot where your initial reaction might be to run off the pack, seeking safety on the top cushion or a snooker behind the black, can be seen in figure 52, shot A.

It beats me why so many players go for this, because unless you judge it perfectly and get the snooker, you only leave your opponent a chance to run away off the pack to safety himself. Anyway, the escape is not hard, with an easy shot off the side cushion. This probably puts you in a far tougher spot than you put him.

Cut out this step. Just trickle the white into the pack — and wait for your opponent to try the snooker off the pack behind the black. Shot B is far more likely to pay dividends.

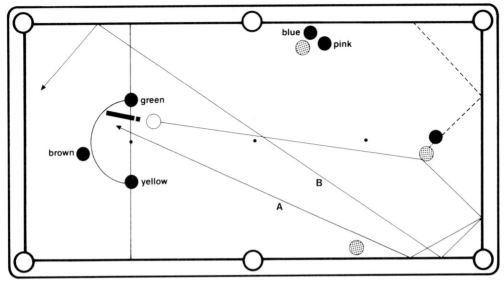

Figure 53

CHOICE OF SAFETY

It is possible in figure 53 to play safe off any one of the three remaining reds. The choice of safety shot depends on the state of the game. If you have a good lead, you will not want to move the lone red on the side cushion. The fact that this red is safe can prevent your opponent building a break. For the same reason, you will not want to move the red next to the pink and blue, for fear of bringing colours into the open and making them more pottable.

The pick of the reds in this situation, then, is the red closest to black. The red cannons onto black and the black runs safe towards the side cushion or even onto it. This makes it very hard indeed for your opponent to score heavily off the remaining reds. Of course, if you are the player trailing on the scoreboard, you will be playing the opposite strategy and trying to move reds and high-scoring colours out into the open.

As with a number of the safety shots we will look at in the next few pages, you might use plain ball or side, depending on the position of the balls. This you will have to experiment with.

Shot A is plain ball; shot B is played with side. Shot B would be the preferred one, depending on how the baulk colours were placed.

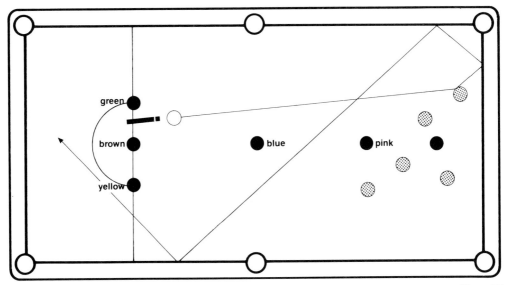

Figure 54

PACE IS THE ACE

You are playing on a table which doesn't inspire confidence, and you are not sure how much roll-off there might be on a slow-moving safety shot. Get the shot wrong in figure 54, and you could be sitting down for the next few minutes while your opponent has a field day.

The answer here, rather than trying a straight up-and-down run on the white, is to go around the angles. This path allows you to hit the cue ball harder, so cancelling out any chance of it veering from its path. An added advantage with this shot is that you can even over-hit it and make the shot too strong. The white is travelling across the table, so it won't go back down on the reds.

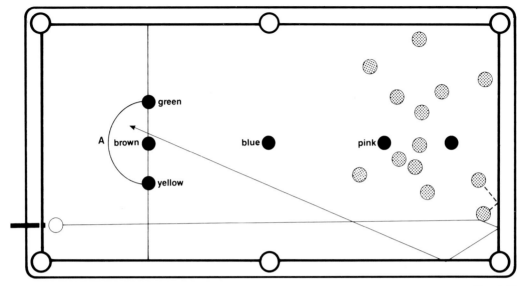

Figure 55

BEST BEHIND THE BROWN

The top end of the table has measles in figure 55! Your opponent has you in a spot, with the cue ball close to the baulk rail. As you look for a safety reply, bear in mind that the target area for the cue ball is behind the brown.

A centrally-placed cue ball, left roughly in the area marked A, reduces your opponent's chances of himself clipping a red and running back to baulk with his next shot. Even if you don't manage to make the prime area — as we have failed to do in this example — it is better to make the reply tougher for your opponent than it would have been if you had just clipped a red and run the white down the yellow side of baulk.

When the boot is on the other foot and you find yourself in this position — with the cue ball centrally in baulk and no clear safety route available — it's sometimes better to go all out for the pot.

Try to work out which is harder: the safety or the pot. Once you make your mind up to go for the pot, go for it with 100 per cent concentration. Don't worry about position. All your attention must be riveted on the pot.

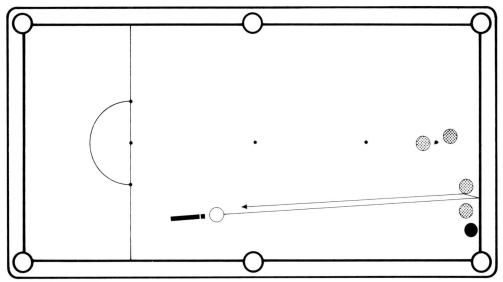

Figure 56

CUSHION-FIRST SAFETY I

A useful option when the straightforward clip-and-run safety shot looks dangerous is to play cushion-first.

It is hard to miss the red in figure 56 when you play off the cushion. The only slightly difficult part is to clip it thin enough so that the cue ball still has enough pace to travel back down the table.

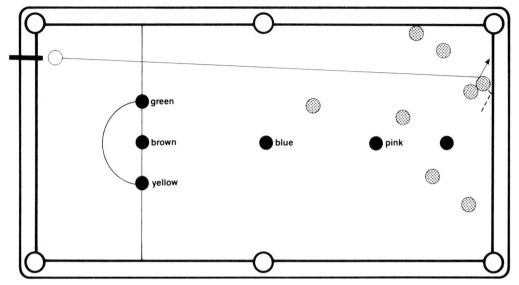

Figure 57

DON'T BE OBSSESSED WITH BAULK

It's hard, in figure 57, to get the cue ball back behind the low colours — so don't try! A roll-up to the red on the top cushion leaves your opponent no potting chance. It does, of course, give him a reply that begs for a return safety into baulk. Still, there is always the chance that he will miscalculate, move a red and give you an easier shot next time.

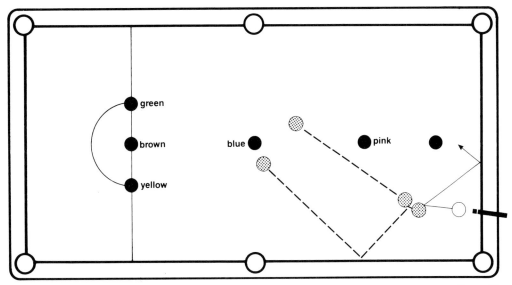

Figure 58

TWO-IN-ONE SAFETY

Two reds are left in figure 58. You could play thin off one of them to put your opponent in baulk. But if you don't snooker him, you will leave a possible pot into the top pocket.

Alternatively, by playing one red onto the other, you push both reds down the table, while a little screw shot adds to the fun by putting the cue ball behind the black.

This kind of shot is good if you have a fair lead and your opponent needs a couple of high-value balls plus the colours to win. By playing the shot stronger, you can push the reds well down the table to make it really tough for him to get position on the high colours. Devious, eh?

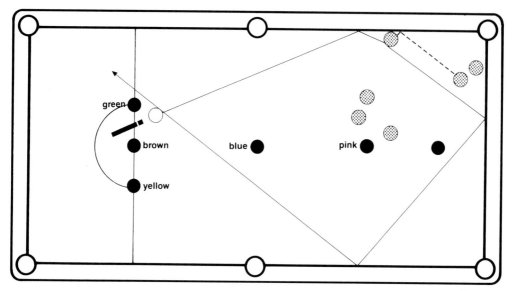

Figure 59

CUSHION-FIRST SAFETY II

Figure 59 shows a very tricky position. There appears to be no escape route to safety — but look again. By playing cushion-first, you alter the angle onto the side-cushion red and run round off the angles to return to baulk.

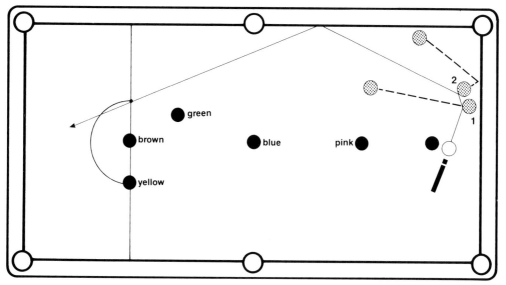

Figure 60

SHOOT FOR THE POSITIVE SAFETY

There is a bit of a problem in figure 60, but there is a neat way out. No pot is available and if you try to play safe off red 2, you don't have enough of an angle to get the white down the table without striking the red hard. In that case, the red will go down the table with the white. One way is to roll up to red, but all your opponent needs to do then is play a good safety shot down the table.

The best shot here is to play a cannon off red 1 onto red 2, to send white down the table. This way, you have created a much wider angle and so don't have to strike the cue ball so hard. You have cancelled the risk of the reds running too far and the cue ball should run away cleanly and some distance.

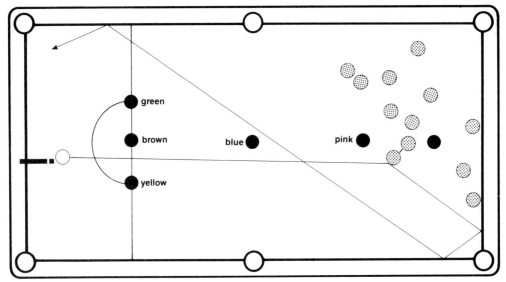

Figure 61

PUT ATTACK INTO YOUR DEFENCE

It may sound contradictory, but you should try to make your safety play as attacking as you can. Before you automatically get down to play a clip-and-run safety shot off a red and back down to baulk, see if there's a chance to be more aggressive. Figure 61 is a good example.

Hit the cue ball with right-hand side to send it off three cushions and into baulk in the area of the green pocket. This leaves your opponent with a very difficult shot — far more difficult than a clipped safety, which he can simply do back to you.

Remember that, generally speaking, it is harder for your opponent to play across the face of another ball to gain safety than it is for him just to clip-and-run.

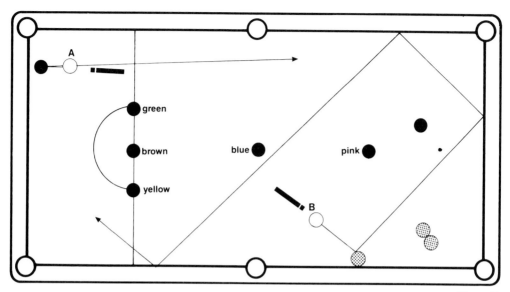

Figure 62

SAFETY AT THE DOUBLE

The double-kiss can be a useful safety shot. Shot A in figure 62 has the red touching the cushion, with white almost directly behind it. By playing the red full-ball with a touch of bottom, you can screw back. No great speed or power is needed here. A slow or gentle shot will still double-kiss and screw back the length of the table.

The fact that the red has nowhere to go, being trapped on the cushion, gives the cue ball extra energy. The effect is similar to playing the white off a cushion.

Shot B can be used to get out of tricky situations. Aim at the part of the object ball that is farthest from the cushion. You get the double-kiss and the white will rebound around the angles for safety. You can experiment with these shots using left or right-hand side.

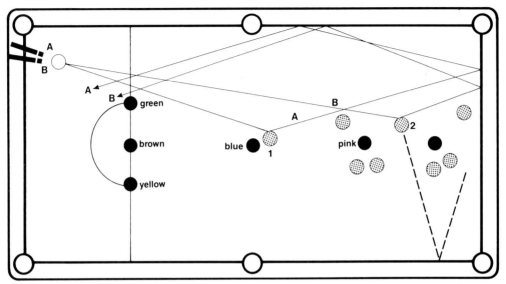

Figure 63

NEAR OR FAR FOR SAFETY?

Most of the time when playing a safety shot, it is better and easier to play off the nearest red. This helps cancel out unintentional side on the cue ball and leaves little to chance on a dodgy table. However, this is a guide-line, not a rule.

In figure 63 you can see that it might be easier to play safe off red 1, but there might be more profit in playing off red 2 instead. With the cue ball back in baulk off red 2, your opponent is under greater pressure to produce a good safety shot in reply. Unless he moves red 1 with his shot, it is lurking in the middle of the table for you to scoop up if he fluffs his response.

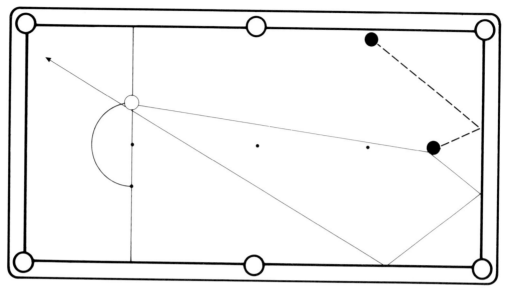

Figure 64

ALL ON THE RESPOTTED BLACK

There's a fairly predictable pattern in most matches, when the frame is drawn and the black is respotted. Most players will take one of two courses if they win the toss. Either they put their opponent on the table and hope he fluffs the shot as he hits the black down the spots for safety, or has a go himself at hitting the black down the spots for safety.

I usually elect to break if I win the toss, and I think I have a better chance of forcing the issue by not playing the 'standard' shot. I hit the black quarter-ball, with no side on the cue ball. Figure 64 shows how the black goes off top and side cushions and the white runs off two cushions into baulk. When you think about it, even the well-played 'standard' shot leaves you a similar safety shot in reply, but from the other end of the table.

I am trying to leave my opponent a difficult safety shot, or tempt him into trying a very difficult pot. Even if I cannot get the black tight against the cushion, the long pot is doubly difficult for him: it's a long pot and the pressure is twice as bad because it's a black ball game.

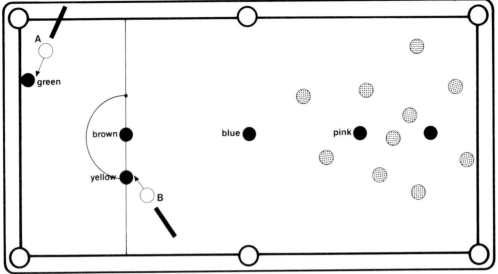

Figure 65

JUST PLAIN AWKWARD

You have just taken a red and didn't get the position you hoped for. With no colour on, you can try the next best thing to a snooker, by making your opponent's next shot downright difficult. Shots A and B in figure 65 show the idea.

If you just roll up to the front of the object ball, you leave the opponent with extremely awkward bridging.

This can produce as good a result as a snooker trickled off the object ball and behind one of the baulk colours. Sometimes it is even better than a snooker, because you force your opponent to play directly at a red. It's going to be tough for him to be accurate with the difficult bridging and cueing, and by not snookering him, you have given him no excuse for half-trying the escape with a return to safety in mind.

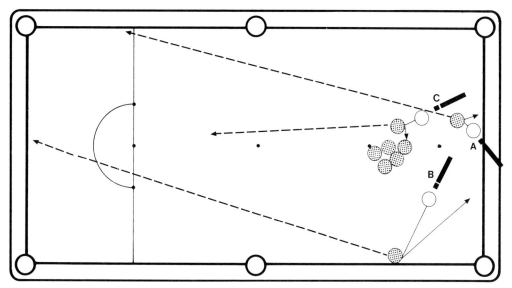

Figure 66

THE SAFETY-STOPPER

Your safety game might not be that hot, or you may simply prefer potting and attacking. This can be very frustrating if you find yourself up against a hit-and-run merchant, who wants to scoop up his red and colour, then keep running down into the 'long grass'. You can limit his choices by taking the opportunity to push a red or two down the table when you have a chance, as in figure 66.

Don't clip the red and run down for safety. Instead, push the red downtable, as in shot A, and make your opponent think twice about running off the pack to play safe again.

A similar situation occurs in shot B. Sending the red down into baulk doesn't exactly kill any safety ideas that your opponent may have, but it certainly makes life more difficult for him.

Shot C is even better. Pop that loose red from the edge of the pack down to the middle of the table and leave him behind the bunched reds. In this way, you can limit his next safety shot to the top of the table, where openings are more likely.

This strategy works well if your safety game is off, and you find you are hitting too thick or too thin. You are forcing the game to be played at shorter distances, which might allow you to get your eye in better.

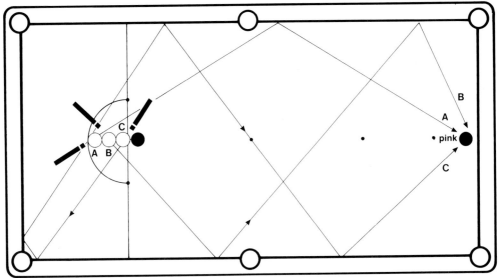

Figure 67

TIGHT IS RIGHT

Figure 67 shows how important it is to get the cue ball as tight as possible to the intervening ball.

Shot A, with the cue ball just two balls' distance from the black, allows a shot off one cushion to strike pink.

Shot B, one ball's width away, toughens the shot quite a bit. There is no angle to play off one cushion, so it has to be a two-cushion escape.

Shot C, right on the black, gives maximum problems to your opponent. It is a four-cushion route this time, and this means it's at least four times harder than if you had left it in position A.

It does not follow that you always want your opponent to miss. If you are ten points behind, you might be better leaving him shot A, half-hoping that he'll make contact and set you up with the pink, and then black for game. If he were faced with shot C, he would probably miss but leave you no pot. He has conceded only six points, and would still be four ahead, needing just one ball to win.

It is a matter of tactics how tight you lay the snooker. Generally, though, it's good policy to think in terms of the tighter the better.

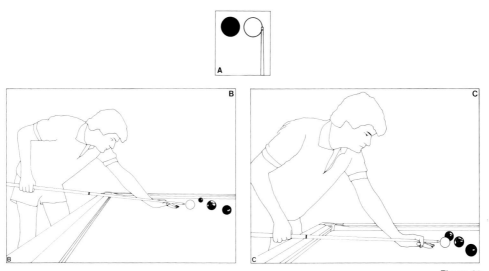

Figure 68

FINDING THE RIGHT TOUCH

When you are playing tight snookers or trying to escape from situations where balls are almost touching, you have to develop techniques to avoid the push shot. It is a foul, of course, if your cue tip is still in contact with the cue ball when the white makes contact with another ball. Figure 68 shows three ways of developing this deft touch and avoiding the push.

Diagram A shows how to address the cue ball when it and the object ball are very close. Approach the white from the side, so that you're playing across the shot instead of into it. Think of it as playing a miscue on the side opposite the object ball. The white is thrown sideways into the other ball, but your tip will have cleared the cue ball before it makes contact.

Diagram B shows a way of improving your weight in roll-up shots. A lot of players have trouble with these and you might find your control is better if you alter your grip. If you find that you frequently under-hit, and maybe even foul on this kind of roll-up shot, move your grip about a third of the way down the cue. You'll probably get a better feel of the stroke, especially if you move your bridge hand closer to the cue ball. It can also help if you stand upright.

Diagram C shows a method for the very shaky player, to ensure that he does not follow through and foul. Resting the cue on the cushion rail, move the tip of the cue close to the cue ball. Grip the cue so that your fingers are actually touching the cushion rail. Use the looped bridge to prevent the cue rising. As you make the stroke, use the rail to prevent your hand going through any farther. You are using the edge of the table as a buffer for your hand, and there is no way that you can follow through and make a push shot.

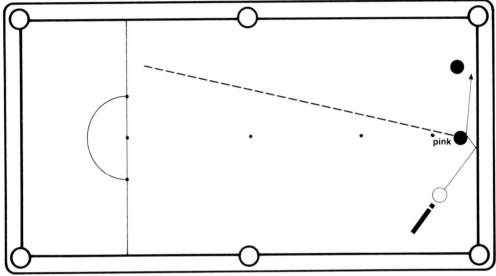

Figure 69

CUSHION-FIRST SNOOKER

You are 14 points behind with pink and black left: a snooker is needed. The cushion-first snooker will do the trick, as you can see in figure 69.

Coming off the top cushion first, punch the pink downtable and look to run the cue ball behind the black. If it drops perfectly, you make the snooker. If not, you have at least made the next shot tough.

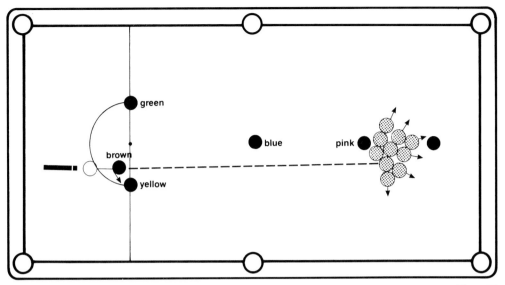

Figure 70

PUNCH PRODUCES PROFIT

A lot of players, faced with the play in figure 70, would roll the white up behind the brown to get the snooker. This has drawbacks. All the reds are grouped and present a pretty big target for your opponent to aim for. He can simply run up the table slowly to make contact with the pack or, if he misses, give you four points but no further great advantage.

You will profit more from this situation if you punch the brown up the table to open up the reds, stunning behind the yellow for the snooker. This way you are likely to gain the initiative, whether your opponent rolls up or misses. You might have disturbed a pottable red or two into the open.

I would still advocate this kind of attacking safety if the snooker behind the yellow were not on. Even if all you could achieve were a screwback to send brown into the reds and put the white down on the bottom cushion, it's likely to be more lucrative than the obvious roll-up to the brown.

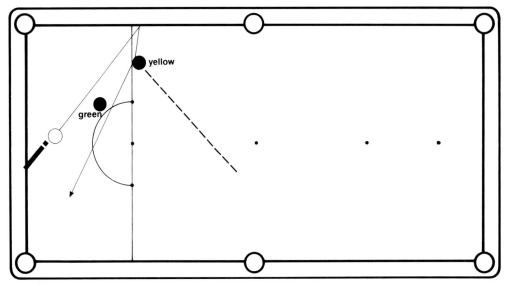

Figure 71

ESCAPE ROUTES: THINK POSITIVE

I presume from the fact that you're reading this book that you feel reasonably confident about working out simple, one-cushion escapes from snookers. I suggest that you now address yourself, when faced with these shots, to a more advanced method that entails not just getting out of the snooker, but thinking beyond that. In figure 71, I show an example of the thinking approach to these escapes.

The plain-ball escape is risky, because both balls could finish in the open. The aiming point for this one-cushion escape is farther up the table than the natural angle, and the stroke is played with left-hand side. The side brings the cue ball into the yellow at an angle that sends the yellow up the table and the cue ball back into baulk.

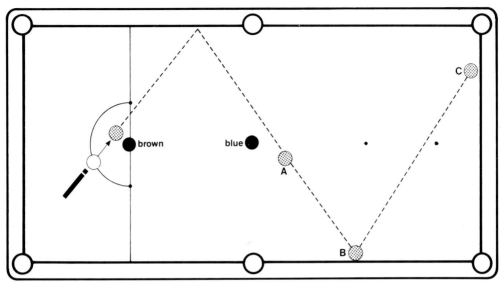

Figure 72

LET YOUR BRAIN TAKE THE STRAIN

Snookering is not just the business of tying up your opponent and getting points on the scoreboard if he misses contact with the ball on. It's about creating openings for your own next shot. Look at the situation in figure 72.

I'm surprised how many players would not think beyond the simple stun behind the brown to guarantee the snooker. As I said earlier in this chapter, you should certainly be aiming to put the cue ball as tight as you can on the snookering ball, but there is another objective with this kind of shot.

You must think where the object ball, in this case a red, is going to finish. You could, with the right strength, place it at any point along the path indicated.

Put the red on or close to the points marked B on the side cushion, or C on the top cushion, and you have made your opponent's response nowhere near as worrying for him as it should be. He can plan his escape by simply rolling up to positions B or C in the knowledge that if he misses he has not left you on.

You can make his life more difficult (and isn't that one of the aims of the game?) by running the red through to position A. Here, he cannot roll up to it for fear of leaving it on. He has to play with some strength, knowing that if he hits it he has little control of what he leaves you after that. If he misses it, he might give away a free ball, or at least leave the red out in the open and available when it's your turn.

Why be just difficult, when with a little more thought and effort you can be downright nasty?

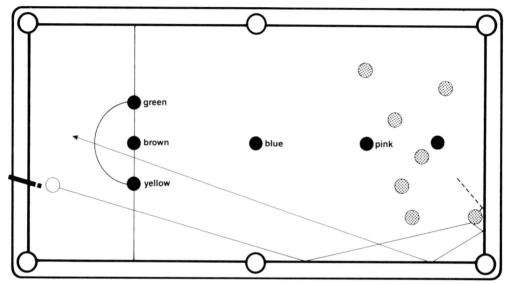

Figure 73

THE THREE-CUSHION RETURN

Striking a red in figure 73 takes little trouble but there's lots of danger if things go wrong. Look for the positive approach to this kind of dilemma.

This is not an easy shot, but you've been forced into the three-cushion escape and return to baulk by a good shot from your opponent. Play off the side cushion with extreme bottom right-hand side to clip the red away from the top cushion. The spin on the cue ball will mean it will return down the table with running side and, if luck is with you, back into baulk for safety or even another snooker.

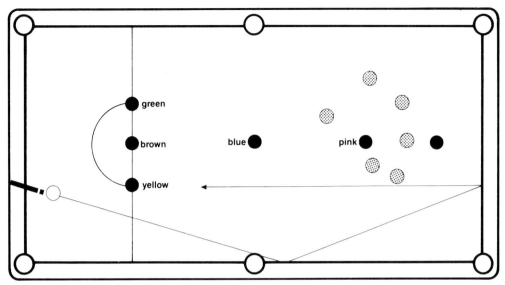

Figure 74

THE PRO WAY OUT OF A SNOOKER

You might have wondered, as you watch top-flight players, why they choose a path out of a snooker that seems to limit their chances of making contact with an object ball. Perhaps it is not such a mystery these days, with such expert commentary on TV, whereby 'whispering men' behind the microphones can explain to the uninitiated what is happening. However, as a player yourself, you might want to understand a little better the thinking process behind the kind of shot illustrated by figure 74.

There shouldn't be much trouble hitting a red in this situation, right? Right, but a plain ball shot which gives you contact with a red is also likely to leave your opponent thinking it's his birthday. With all those reds and big colours available, he ought to have you keeping your seat warm for quite a few minutes.

The shot to go for is off two cushions with right-hand side. After contact with the top cushion, the white comes straight back down the table. If you make contact with a red, the cue ball is more likely to continue down the table — and if you miss, you have greatly reduced the risk of a 'leave'.

Never aim to miss the red — that's against the rules. Still, it does make more sense to minimise the danger if the shot does not work perfectly. It certainly makes more sense than clattering in among those loose reds and presenting your opponent with dozens of points.

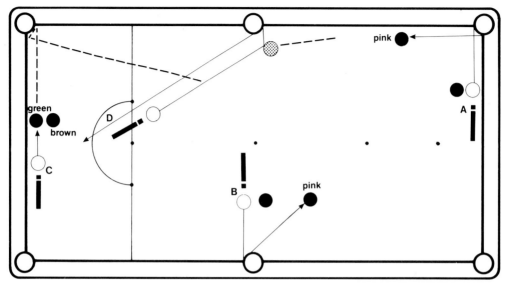

Figure 75

JAWS 1, 2, 3 AND 4

One way of getting out of snookers that is often overlooked, is to use the jaws of the pockets as the apex of your escape route.

In shot A in figure 75 you don't have a lot of option. You are on pink, which is on the side cushion, but the cue ball is hugging both black and the top cushion. You will foul unless you play away from the black and the only clear path is along the angles created by the opening around the top pocket. Shot A is hit onto the far jaw to rebound across the drop of the pocket, onto the other jaw and down the side cushion.

This is a useful shot to have in your repertoire, and with practice and in less congested situations, you can vary the angle of deflection to suit different needs.

Shot B is another in which you might find the far jaw of the pocket a useful 'wall' off which to bounce. Using just one jaw this time, you can make the pink.

Shot C shows how you can use the same theory to lay a snooker, too. Stun the white behind the brown and send the green off the jaws and away. Another way you can use the jaws for safety can be seen in shot D — bring white off the middle-pocket opening and back into baulk.

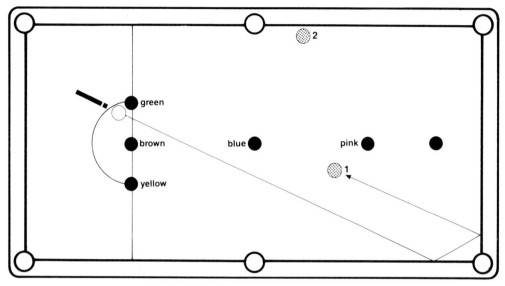

Figure 76

A BETTER CHOICE, HIT OR MISS

The main point to bear in mind when playing out of snookers, is that it is better to miss than set up a red. Again, I am not encouraging you to break the rules or go against the spirit of the game, both of which say that a deliberate miss is not only unsporting but is also a foul shot. But you should go for the escape with the thought that if you miss, you do not set up a loose red or even leave a free ball. It's worth remembering that a miss on a red costs you four points. A bad contact can cost you the frame.

Green and blue are the snookering balls in figure 76. So, do we go for red 1 or red 2? We have a choice. Red 1 is by far the best bet, because even if we make contact and leave it pottable, our opponent will find it tough to clear up with red 2 still tucked against the side cushion.

If the position of the balls forces us into going for red 2, the policy should be to play the cue ball with just enough pace to reach the red. We would want to leave it safe, rather than knock it clear for a possible pot by our opponent.

I would go further and say that even if you can hit red 2, you should try for red 1. It's a brave way to go, but if you miss red 1, you are running back towards baulk and only one red is in the open. Move red 2 badly, and your opponent has two reds out in the open. At top-class level, you could be dead!

9

Superior Strategy and Telling Tactics

A good player will nearly always beat a good potter in the long run. This game is not just about sticking balls away, making positions and building big breaks. Your tactics have to be drawn up in recognition of the fact that you have an opponent to beat and he may be equally good at sticking, making and building.

Let's start this section with a couple of thoughts about when *not* to pot. Take figure 77 as an example of when it is better to shun the pot and play according to the scoreboard.

We have potted the last red and left ourselves on the blue with no angle to go down for the yellow, which is safe on the baulk cushion anyway. The scoreboard tells us we are 21 in front. Now if we pot blue we are 26 ahead. With the blue respotted, all the colours will be just sitting there for a clear-up by our opponent if we fail to keep the yellow safe.

A better shot is to put the blue safe on the side cushion and try for a snooker behind the black. If we get the snooker and the opponent fouls, we are now 25 ahead and need just yellow to win with the blue safe.

If the opponent gets out of the snooker he risks setting yellow up, and all we need is yellow and green to make the frame safe. If he gets out of the snooker and eventually takes yellow and green we are still 16 in front

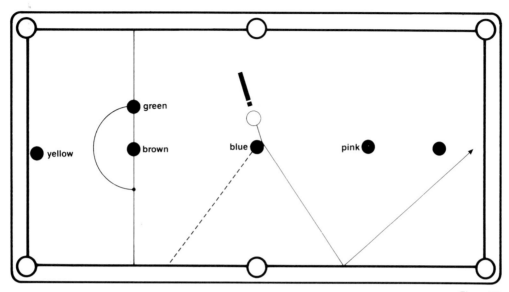

Figure 77

needing only the brown to make the frame. We have thus made ourselves a firm favourite to win the frame by refusing the temptation of the pot.

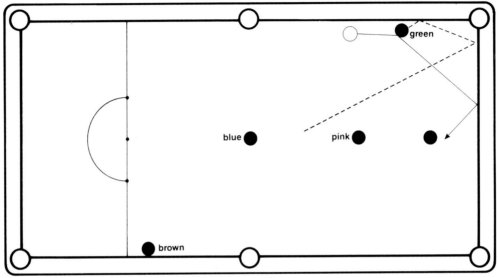

Figure 78

DON'T BE COLOUR-BLINDED

Figure 78 shows the table as we face an easy green with a 17-point lead. This is another situation where it is better strategy to avoid the pot.

All we need is green and brown to make the frame safe. If we pot green, we have little chance of taking brown unless we get perfect positioning or cannon the brown into a pottable position. We could pot green then play safe on the brown, but the frame is likely to go to the first player to make a safety mistake on the brown. The opponent can clear up if he gets a sniff at the brown.

A better tactic is to go for an aggressive snooker from the green, hoping your opponent will give you penalty points. Then all you need is the green to leave your opponent needing snookers.

Even if your opponent pots green before you get a snooker, he's still stuck with the brown on the side cushion. While you go for snookers you might get a chance to cannon blue, pink or black safe — and his chances are limited even more.

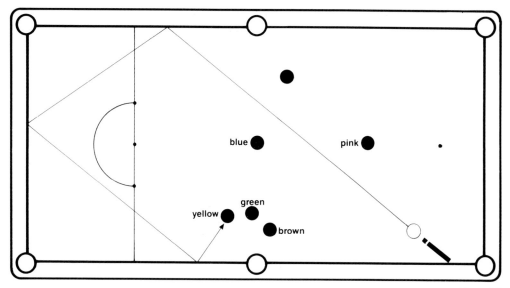

Figure 79

LET THE FORCE BE WITH YOU

The position in figure 79 is that you are snookered behind the green on the yellow. The way the other colours are sitting, it's pointless to just roll up and hit yellow because, if you miss and leave the yellow up or a free ball, a reasonable amateur will clear for game.

By playing with force, even if you don't hit the yellow, you're bound to disturb some of the colours. The chances are that you'll put one or more of them safe or on the cushion, making a clear-up by your opponent unlikely.

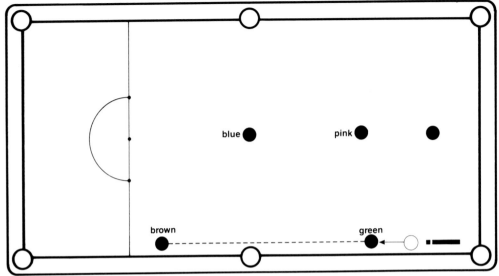

Figure 80

NEEDING ALL THE BALLS

The player facing the situation in figure 80 is 23 behind, and so needs all five colours to win.

If you are in arrears in this way and one of the colours is tied up on the cushion — in this case the brown — roll the green onto the brown if you get the chance. This not only makes it difficult for your opponent to play safe, but also more times than not he will be forced to bring the brown into play. That could make your job of clearing all the balls quite a bit easier.

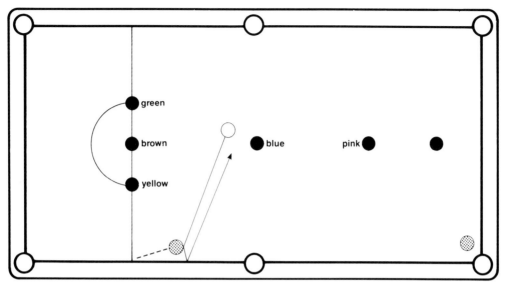

Figure 81

EASING THE PAIN A LITTLE

There are some situations, such as the one in figure 81, where all you can do is minimise the damage that your opponent can do.

You are snookered on the red over the top pocket and there's not much chance of potting the second red. You could lay a snooker on the top red by clipping the second down the cushion and trying to bring the white off the cushion to a point close to where it started. This demands good judgment of weight.

Presuming this snooker does not come off, the red will have been pushed down onto the side cushion, safe, and you trust that you have limited your opponent to a red and colour.

We discuss elsewhere the need to bring reds off the cushion to keep a break going. What we are looking at now is the defensive aspect of that — putting reds and colours in a safe place where the opponent cannot make use of them.

Take another situation where you have a 24-point lead against a good potter. You've taken the last red. The colours are all on their spots except brown, which is tucked against a side cushion. You should be looking to protect your lead by putting another colour safe, and this should be either the green or the blue.

The theory is that it will be difficult for him, good potter or not, to make two outstanding pots on the trot. He might pot the yellow and make the difficult green but would be stretched to cannon out the brown with the same stroke on the green. Then he faces a tough brown with low odds of repeating an outstanding pot.

What happens if you do not make two successive colours safe? Let's say brown is still on the side cushion and you elect to put pink safe. A good pot on the brown could give him a chance at an open blue, with the possibility of moving the pink clear in the stroke with which he takes the blue. Frame over!

10

Useful Rules, OK?

I shudder sometimes when I watch club players and see them throw away good chances; not because they are poor players, but because they do not know enough about the rules of snooker to use them to their advantage.

Pick up a copy of the little book published by the Billiards and Snooker Control Council and study it. It can pay off. In there, you'll find not only the rules that most of us know, but explanations of rules that govern occasions where our ignorance could cost us points and frames.

What, for example, are your options if the referee declares 'angled ball'? Can you *ever* lay a snooker behind a free ball?

This short chapter will deal with one or two common situations where our understanding of the rule book could make the difference between winning a championship match and losing it.

Figure 82 shows the angled-ball position. Your opponent has just fouled and the white has come to rest tight against the jaw of the top pocket. A good referee, having declared foul and given you the penalty points, will announce, 'Angled ball.' You probably know that you can ask your opponent to play again after any foul, whether you are snookered or not, so that's your first option. Your second choice, since you are snookered by the jaw, is to nominate a free ball — but in this instance that would be

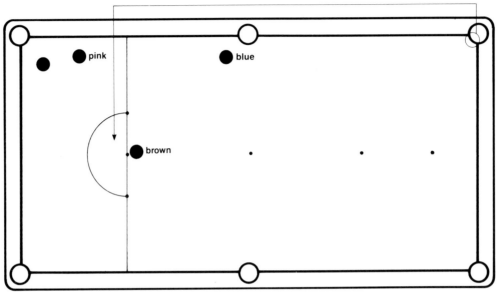

Figure 82

rather daft!

However, you do have a third and vital option open to you under the rules. You can actually tell the referee you want to play from baulk, place the white ball in the D and from there, faced with a situation such as in figure 82, that knowledge and that decision can win you the frame — it should do with the balls in this position.

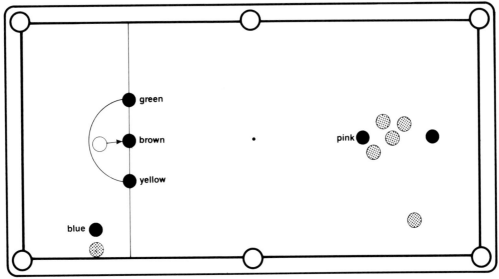

Figure 83

ROLL UP, ROLL UP, IT'S LEGAL

Your opponent has fouled, you are in the D and the next ball is on a red, as in figure 83. You'd love to roll up behind the brown. However, you know that the rule book says you can't lay a snooker behind a free ball unless only pink and black are left on the table. What do you do? You roll up behind the brown and snooker your opponent on the bunch of reds. It's perfectly valid in these circumstances.

It is true that you have snookered him on nearly all the reds by dropping behind the brown, but that single red hiding behind the blue against the side cushion means that the snookering ball for this red is not the nominated free ball. It is a good shot, and legal.

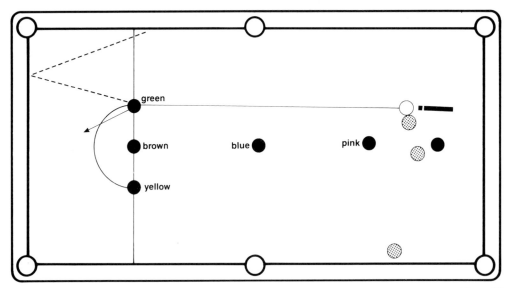

Figure 84

A TOUCHING SITUATION

Some players fail to realise that when the cue ball is touching a red, and red is the ball on, you can play straight onto a colour. It is not a foul shot.

Take the position shown in figure 84. Playing onto a colour like this can move an open ball into a safe position when you have a nice lead, as in this example, or promote a colour into a pottable position if you are trailing. It's all a case of knowing the rules.

Incidentally, it's good strategy to bear in mind whether your opponent is right-handed or left-handed. If he is right-handed, it's better to put green safe; if he's left-handed, yellow safe. The idea is to force him to use the rest if he gets in a position to begin a clearance.

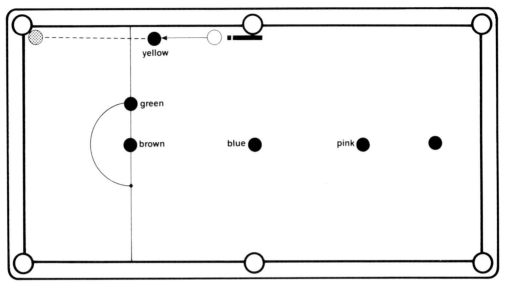

Figure 85

IF IT'S FREE, I'LL HAVE IT

One final example of making the rules work in your favour. After a foul by your opponent, you are of course entitled to a free ball if you are snookered. Many players forget — or never even knew — that you can use this free ball to pot a ball on.

For example, the frame is down to the colours and your opponent fouls on yellow. You are snookered and select blue as your free ball. You can use the blue to cannon onto the yellow and pot it. You are now on green. (Incidentally, it is not a foul even if the blue goes in too. You simply score two points, the blue is respotted and your next ball is green.)

Understanding this will help you in situations such as figure 85. After a foul, your opponent has left you snookered behind the yellow with the remaining red sitting over the bottom pocket.

Many players will ask the opponent to play again, trusting that he will play off the opposite side cushion and miss the red. This, to my mind, is too risky. It's not a tough shot for him, and the chances are that if he hits the red, he will pot it. Then we're really up against it, if he can take a colour and somehow get the yellow back into play.

A far better decision is to nominate yellow as the free ball, so for the purpose of this shot the yellow becomes a red. Use it to pot the red. You leave the yellow over the pocket and sink it with your next shot. Yellow respots. As long as you can get from the potted yellow to the respotted yellow, you could be on for a clearance.

All it takes is knowing what the rules are and how to use them. With two players of more-or-less equal playing ability, the one who uses his head as well as his cue is more likely to win through to the next round of the tournament. And you will have done it with the help of the rule book.

11

Milestones, Mettle and Matches

All good books on snooker pass on advice about cues, tips, etc. I would like to reinforce this for the non-beginner in passing but not to dwell on it. There are other important matters which I have not seen dealt with in any depth elsewhere. These cover such things as how and what to practise, how to stay in control of yourself during a game and how to approach the nerve-wracking big match.

The topics here arise out of the questions I get asked most often by players at all levels as they seek to improve their game to the maximum of their potential. These final chapters do not advise you about the way to pot balls, but more about how to get the vital psychological approach right, to get you in better shape to approach matches and win them. Let's begin by seeing where your standards are now, and how far you have to go — or want to go.

THE MILESTONES

You should realise that a person's highest break is no real reflection of his ability. I have known a number of players who can claim some pretty impressive high breaks, especially in practise, but who can't string three or four balls together in a match, and lose more than they win.

So as we talk now about standards, I would like you to disregard your highest break, and honestly put yourself in the category which is decided by the breaks you make *regularly* and *consistently*.

STAGE 1 (BREAKS 1 TO 25)

At this standard, you are either a beginner, or your cue action is deplorable — probably both.

If you are a beginner, take heart, because you already have something in common with Steve Davis and the rest of us — we were all at the same stage once.

If you are not a beginner, it means your cueing is probably way off. Before you even start to practise seriously, you must seek out your local coach. You need major surgery on your stance and cue action, and until you get these right you'll be wasting time even thinking about practice.

While we're talking about stage 1, it is probably worthwhile to pause for a moment or two and talk about cues.

Thousands of players, probably hundreds of thousands of players, are dissatisfied with their cues because the perishing things won't pot balls of their own accord!

When the cue is in one of those devilish moods and refuses to pot, we tend to put it down to the fact that it is too thick and short. Or thin and long. Or stiff. Or whippy. Or light. Or heavy. I could go on.

Somewhere in the world, we are convinced, there is a cue made for us individually. It will fulfil all our dreams of what a cue should be, it will be tailor-made to fit us, perfectly balanced to suit us and a paragon of perfection that is guaranteed to make us play well.

The sad fact is that, if we ever came across this magic wand, we would probably discard it and continue the search for one that is not so thick and short, thin and long, etc. Keep looking for this supreme hunk of wood, and you will have more anguish than Jason did in his search for the Golden Fleece.

To play snooker at all seriously, you *must* have your own cue.

So, you are deciding on a new cue, either for the first time or to replace your old one. Ask a coach or a top player at your club for some advice on the general guidelines to bear in mind when you shop. This is as close as you're going to get to the Land of the Promised Cue.

Try to avoid the local general sports shop, where you might be lucky to find a dozen cues in a rack between the aerobics outfits and the running spikes. Phone round the big-name snooker firms to ask if any have an on-site billiard table on which to test the cues — some do. Buying a cue without testing it is akin to borrowing someone else's dentures to eat dinner — they won't fit and they won't work. And they certainly won't feel comfortable.

As you enter your chosen store, you will be met by a gracious assistant, who probably knows quite a bit about snooker cues — particularly which ones carry the biggest commission for him. He will wax lyrical about the quality of hand-spliced and expensive cues. He will stress the absolutely essential nature of expensive cue-tipping equipment. He will be intent to persuade you that you also need an expensive name-brand cue case, chalk-holder and all manner of vital utensils such as files for roughing up tips, and the things that get stones out of horses' hooves. Tell him politely that you want to look and you'll let him know when you've found something, thank you.

Stand in front of the racks of cues, bringing to mind what the coach told you about which weight, length and ferrule size suit you, and this will narrow the choice down — down to only a few hundred!

At this stage, you have to rely on the 'feel' of cues. Pick them up, and try as many as you like. Take a lot of time if you need to. The only thing I would advise is that you ignore the price tag, if you can afford to. Price is no guarantee that you have found your one-and-only magic wand. When you've chosen the cue, it's worth asking the assistant if there's any discount — sometimes you get lucky.

OK, you're back at the club and eager to try the cue some more. But before you play with it, you'll probably have to have it retipped. If you do not feel competent, there's usually someone around the club who will re-tip it for a nominal fee. Most of the tips supplied by cue manufacturers are not good, and top pros would have trouble winning an amateur tournament if they played with a cue carrying its original tip. Most professionals go for Blue Diamond or Elk Master.

If your new cue doesn't pot balls by remote control, worry not. It can take at least two or three months for the two of you to grow accustomed to each other!

I presume that you will be following the advice on cue care that you will have read elsewhere, such as not leaning it against a wall but laying it flat or hanging it upright; using a damp cloth to clean it and not sandpaper; and not subjecting the cue to extremes of climate which will cause it to split or warp.

STAGE 2 (BREAKS 26 TO 39)

Congratulations! If you are regularly and consistently making breaks in this area, you are now better than half the players in the world. That's not a bad feeling, is it? You are gradually whittling away the field on your way to becoming World Champion.

Now you have reached stage 2, you are beginning to understand something about the secrets of the game, such as the effects of side, stun and screw. Your problem is almost certainly that you do not have total control over them nearly all the time. Regular practice is what you need, because it is not too big a step to reach stage 3.

STAGE 3 (BREAKS 40 TO 69)

This is the tough one. You can consider yourself a pretty good player because you have achieved a standard which very few ever accomplish. But I must warn you that you can expect to be at stage 3 for quite a long time. Indeed, you may never move out of it.

To have reached this stage, for some people, is just reward for extremely hard work. Others who are luckier, may have reached this point without quite so much dedication and have relied on their natural ability. Whichever applies to you, you are going to find this stage one of the toughest barriers to break through. You are going to have to practise like mad, study the game, practise like mad, play with and learn from better players, practise like mad, read about snooker, and practise like mad!

STAGE 4 (BREAKS 70 TO 99)

There will be some people reading this who have spent a lot of time in stage 3. They have been wondering if they will ever make the step to the stage just below the magic 'ton'.

It's a smaller step from stage 3 to stage 4 than it was from stage 2 to stage 3, and you made that one. So there's no reason why you can't join the ranks of the regular 70, 80 and 90-men provided that you have natural ability tied into sound cue action, dedication and perseverance.

For players in stage 4, the fight really begins. I feel that it is at this point that the hard-working player tends to get left behind. No matter how much dedication you have, it has to be married to God-given ability. Natural talent begins to play a far bigger role at this level of the game.

It is also a sobering thought that even if you are making these kinds of breaks every other time you go to the table, you are not even halfway to a professional career.

STAGE 5 (BREAKS OVER 100)

What can I say? It's a fantastic achievement. You are now a century-plus player and you have got there by means of talent coupled with dedication and a thirst to learn. Only now can you think about making a career out of snooker.

A lot of players in this bracket are only about two blacks off the standard of the lowest professionals. Fourteen points might not sound a lot, but I can assure you that it is. Even with hard training and your natural gift, finding these extra two blacks will probably take you two years.

So the next couple of years are crucial for the player at stage 5. Remember that, strictly speaking, we are thinking in terms of raising your game by one point every two months. These points can be picked up with improvements in your match temperament, concentration and will to win. Much can go wrong, but if you are aware of the pitfalls, you'll be better equipped to understand and handle them.

Frustration is one of the biggest problems. A whole year passes and you expect to have picked up the seven points you need to stay on track. It is easy to find yourself actually playing seven points worse than you were a year earlier. This is one of the maddening, but intriguing aspects of snooker.

You could be going through a bad patch and must be ready to accept that it happens, even to the very best players. Don't tell yourself that you're not going to make it just because you haven't improved a measly seven points in a year. Remind yourself that you've come a long way and, looking back, you played through bad patches before and still clawed your way into stage 5.

The worst thing you can do is conclude that, if you can't improve just seven points after a whole year of sweat, you should throw in the towel. This is one of the psychological barriers through which you have to go. You have the talent and the dedication — that must keep you going. Don't let self-doubt creep in.

A second major problem, after frustration on the table, concerns social pressures away from the table. Amateur snooker at the top standard is very much a young man's game. The explosion of interest over recent years has seen the top players bursting through to the senior ranks at younger and younger ages.

Most of the top-notch players picked up a cue at the age of 12 or even younger, so by the time they reached stage 5 they were around the age of 16 or 17 — about school-leaving age for many. Up to this point, a young player's social life has probably been relatively simple and inexpensive. It revolves round the local cafe, friends' houses and the odd soccer match.

The crunch for the snooker player comes if he leaves school. Suddenly, the 'simple' life disappears. His friends get jobs that bring in money which, compared to their previous pocket-money income, is a small fortune. The bigger pay packets mean that the young snooker player's friends are turning out in the latest fashions, going to discos, finding girlfriends — all of which are out of the grasp of the young player.

It's decision time. And it's a decision that can affect the rest of his life. Does he get a job like his friends, do an honest day's work and enjoy the financial fruits in his leisure time? None of this leaves much room for snooker. Or does he stick with it, sure in the knowledge that he is a good player, but with doubts about how good, and how far he can go? The late teens are a tender age for a person to have this kind of decision facing him. It has to be a mature decision, and one that he shouldn't take alone.

These two — frustration on the table and social pulls away from it — are just examples of the problems that will beset you throughout your playing career. Sometimes the problem is basically mental and can be resolved if you can call upon your own strong character. Sometimes the problem is simply money, and the support of parents, wife and family. Sometimes you cannot be supported by your family. Perhaps you live alone, and expenses such as food and rent have to be met. Some kind of work has to be done to pay for these.

It's very easy for the ordinary working man to look with envy at the top players on TV and object to the vast sums they earn from their ability to pot balls into holes with a piece of wood! But what you are seeing is the icing on the cake for a lucky few. There are more than 100 professionals on the UK list, and the vast majority of them are just as envious of the vast fortunes picked up by the very top people.

Every single professional, whether number 1 or number 120, has got where he has through years of self-denial, heartbreak and disappointment. On an even more sombre note, some of the players I know could not handle the pressure and turned to — or caused — alcoholism, family splits, mental breakdown and even suicide.

When you see these stage 5-plus players, you must remember that they have diced with much peril on the way. (To these stars, I would also say that they should think of the people they saw going down as they made their way up and remember that there, but for the grace of God, go they.)

These, then, are the six stages of snooker, from 1 to 5-plus. Moving from one stage to the next is not easy. Let's not pretend that it is. However, you do get out of snooker what you put in. The reward for the talented and dedicated is not just fame and fortune, but knowing that you have achieved your potential. For the hundreds of thousands of players who don't make it to the top, there can still be this satisfaction.

12

Practice, Practice, Practice

'Nothing in the world can take the place of persistence. Talent will not — nothing is more common than unsuccessful men with talent. Genius will not — unrewarded genius is almost a proverb. Education will not — the world is full of educated derelicts.'

Calvin Coolidge

I would be a very rich man indeed if I had a penny for every person I have heard say: 'If he had practised, he could have been a professional'. As sure as the yellow's worth two points, it is impossible for anyone to become a professional snooker player without thousands of hours spent at the practice table.

I get a lot of questions about practice, and I will run through them here, with answers which I hope will benefit you.

Question: How should I practise?
Answer: Well, any time spent at a table hitting balls is better than no practice. But to get the maximum advantage from the time you're spend-

ing, the first thing is to make sure that the practice table is suitable.

By this I mean practising on a table with generous pockets. First, because it's no fun to keep seeing the ball rattle in the jaws and come out. Second, because tight pockets also restrict some pots along the cushions and limit some of the positional practice strokes you want to play.

I remember reading somewhere about the saying that bad tables breed bad players. It's true, and I feel that larger pockets make it easier for you to learn the art of break-building. Potting balls increases your confidence, which is a major factor in playing well.

Also, try to choose a fast table for practice, provided that the cloth on your club table still has some nap left on it. If the cloth is shiny and bare it will be fast, but you'll find it difficult to control the balls. A fast table with nap on the cloth will, again, help develop your break-building and give you a smooth cue action.

These two ingredients — pockets that are not too tight and a fast-running table — will encourage you to become an attacking type of player. At top level these days, that's what you have to be to survive.

Question: Should I practise alone?

Answer: Yes, if you have the mental fortitude to slog it out on your own. Personally, I mostly practise with someone else — but honestly, it's probably better alone. A couple of hours 'solo flying' gives you the advantage that you can play a variety of shots over and over again until you feel that you have them under control.

The obvious advantage with solo practice is that to get maximum personal benefit out of, say, two hours' worth of practice with someone of your own ability, you have to play for about four hours.

Of the professional players I have heard asked the same question, most agree with me, while one or two will say, 'Not always, but if I play with someone else he's got to be a mug. He also makes a good "ball boy"!' The thinking is obvious. If your practice opponent is several steps below your ability, he is likely to set up authentic game situations which will test your ability to make breaks and clearances. But otherwise, solo practice pays better dividends.

Question: Should I practise safety play?

Answer: Generally, no. For players quite new to the game, I would suggest that for the first two or three years you never play a safety shot in practice. Your table time will be more profitably spent on potting, and building breaks.

A lot of valuable time can be wasted clipping off the pack and putting the cue ball back into baulk. Learn your safety away from the table by watching matches on TV and in the clubs.

You'll find some fun in safety 'games' that will sharpen you up, and there are a few in the chapter on practice. But practising straight safety can be a waste of training time.

Question: What are the pitfalls in practising?
Answer: Not many, really, because practice time is nearly always well spent.

One thing that might appear obvious: don't practise for the sake of practice. If you feel your concentration is slipping or find that you are just knocking balls around, it's better to take a break or stop all together. After this point, you are unlikely to be getting much benefit from the practice anyway.

Another tip is to think out your practice shots better. Occasionally in solo practice, pause and work out whether the shot you're going to play is the right one. I hope that doesn't sound simplistic, but you might be surprised by the number of shots you would have taken because they seemed the easiest or most obvious.

It doesn't matter if you stand at the table for a few minutes working out whether one red would be better than another, or whether position on the pink would be better than black. That's the beauty of practice time, because you don't have an opponent getting fidgety or the referee warning you about time-wasting. Practice time is not just for potting but for practising your shot choice, too.

For example, you have taken the last red and the colours are on their spots. There is no easy colour, but you can go for yellow, green, brown or blue. Try yellow, always. If you go for another colour and miss but get position on the yellow, you've thrown the game away. If you miss the yellow, trying for position on the respotted yellow, the damage is likely to be less.

Another danger in practice might be best illustrated by my turning it into a question for you. If I were to ask you to place the blue on its spot and play the cue ball from hand to practise potting the colour into a top pocket, where would you place the white?

The chances are, if you are right-handed, that you will automatically think of putting the cue ball on or near the yellow spot. Most left-handed players would place it on or near the green spot. Most players show a marked preference for playing a given shot from one side or the other, and this preferred side tends to be dictated by whether they are right-handed or left-handed. It's difficult to offer you a solid reason for this, but it probably has something to do with the eyes.

For example, if I asked a right-handed person to look through a microscope, he would almost certainly use his right eye. If I asked the same person to check the lay of the table after a foul, to see whether my cue ball could squeeze past a colour or whether I am entitled to a free ball, he would probably squat and look along the line of the shot with his left eye closed.

What's the point of this exercise? Well, when you practise solo, it's very easy indeed to practise the things that you do well and avoid the things you find hard. This includes shots which you find easier with a cue-ball approach from the right if you are right-handed, and vice versa for left-handed people. The message I'm trying to put across is that if you are right-handed, you are probably also 'right-eyed'.

Give a little thought to this in your practice routines. After you pot a ball from one angle, set up the same shot on the opposite side of the table and see if you are as confident about making the pot and position from there. You might find that it doesn't work as well and as often. This is something you are going to have to spend some time on.

One final tip about your approach to practice: never practise a pot without playing for position. To do so is to waste the practice time, because all shots except safety and snooker have two halves — the pot and the position. I would go a step further and say that you should practise position onto a certain ball, and not just 'general direction, any colour will do'.

13

'I Don't Know What to Practice'

This is a statement I have heard from many players at many levels. On the following pages I have drawn up several routines to try, and they are in order of playing difficulty so that I can help you get some planning into your practice.

The routines were drawn up to top amateur and professional standards, so if you have not yet reached these stages, you will have to scale down the degree of difficulty in each. For example, routine 1 asks you to pot yellow, green and brown five times. If you are stage 1 or stage 2, your target should be to complete the routine only once or twice.

In most cases I have not indicated where you should place the cue ball to start with — decide yourself, but be ruthless with yourself too.

These routines will be of real benefit to anyone's practice. As you work your way through them, you will have explored every part of the table, potted balls into every pocket using different degrees of side and will have eliminated the trap we talked about earlier, that of practising only the things you can do.

Another plus-factor is that if you work the exercises from start to finish, each time you come to the practice table you can see in your given practice time which exercise you have reached, and how much you have improved. Please don't think, however, that when you start these routines you are entering a race — that's a sure way to fail.

Don't worry, either, if on some days you cannot get past routine 1, because the exercises are not set out simply so that you finish them. If you find that today you only got to routine 3, the practice can still be a success. If you devoted the whole practice time to only three routines, it will have taught you patience. It will also have given you a heavy dose of frustration and helped you control it. Those are two more strings to your bow if you are going to make it to the top.

33 PRACTICE ROUTINES (AND FOUR JUST FOR FUN)

1. Yellow, green and brown on their spots: pot yellow, green and brown five times, playing the white from where it lies after the previous shot.

2. Brown and blue on their spots: pot brown to blue, blue to brown, five times.

3. Black on its spot: pot 20 consecutive blacks from the spot.

4. Pink and black on their spots: pot pink to black, black to pink, five times — but pink must be potted only in middle pockets.

5. Brown and pink on their spots: pot brown to pink, pink to brown, five times.

6. Blue on its spot: pot four consecutive blues, two in the top left-hand pocket, two in the top right-hand pocket.

7. All colours on their spots: clear the colours, and when you get to black get position on the yellow to make a second clearance.

8. Blue on its spot: pot blue in the top left-hand pocket, positioning white to pot blue in the top right, then the middle right and so on clockwise round the pockets.

9. All colours on their spots: clear the colours, but after each pot the cue ball must touch two cushions.

10. Yellow, green, brown and black on their spots: pot yellow to black, black to green, green to black, black to brown.

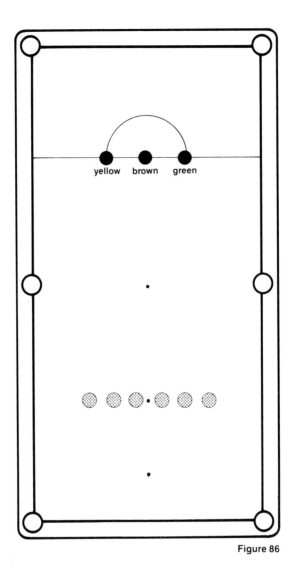

Figure 86

11. Pot all six reds with baulk colours (figure 86).

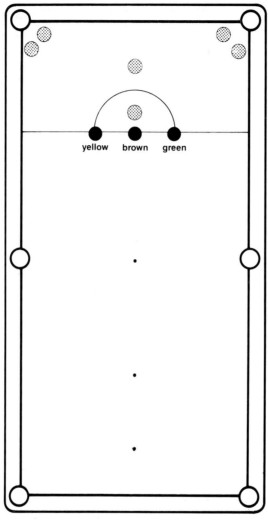

Figure 87

12. Pot all six reds with six baulk colours (figure 87).

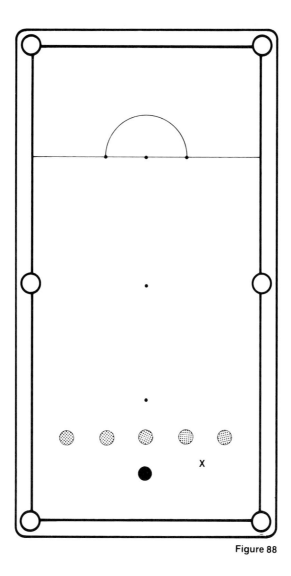

Figure 88

13. Place the cue ball in position X, so that by playing various stun and screw shots it is possible to pot black and cannon all five reds consecutively (figure 88).

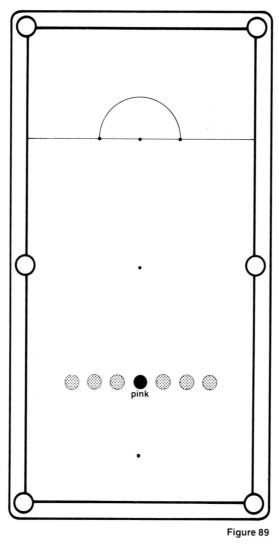

Figure 89

14. Pot six red-pinks (figure 89).

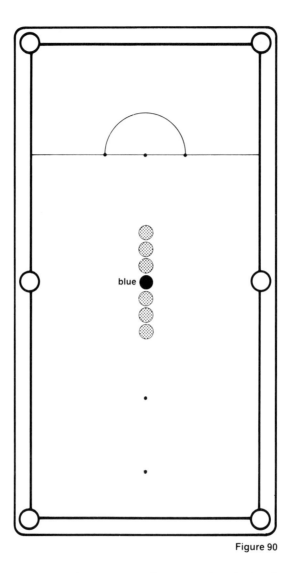

Figure 90

15. Pot six red-blues, but blues must be potted only in the centre pockets (figure 90).

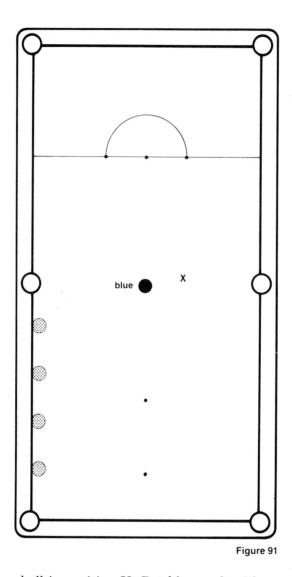

Figure 91

16. Place the cue ball in position X. Pot blue and, with varying degrees of side, make four consecutive cannons on the reds (figure 91).

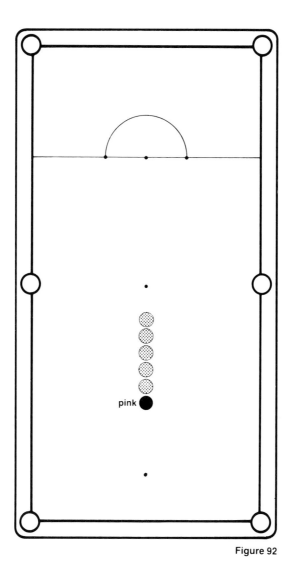

Figure 92

17. Pot five red-pinks (figure 92).

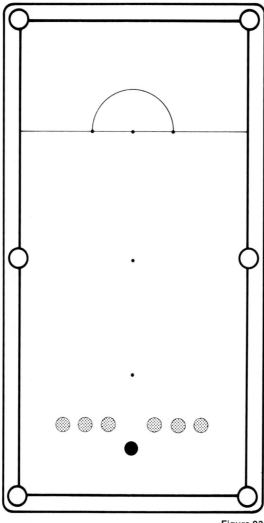

Figure 93

18. Pot six red-blacks (figure 93).

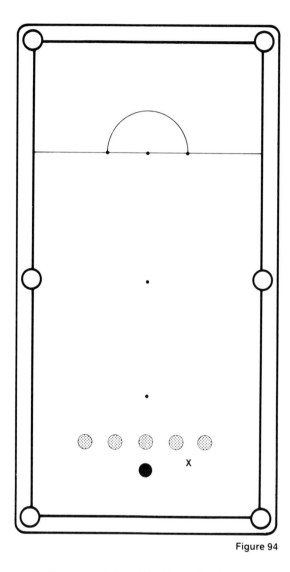

Figure 94

19. Place the cue ball in position X. Pot blacks with varying degrees of screw, stun and side to bring the cue ball off one cushion and make five consecutive cannons on the reds (figure 94).

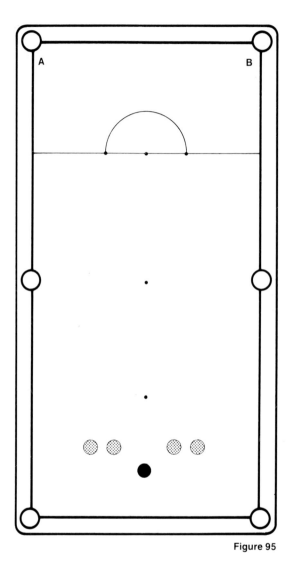

Figure 95

20. Pot four red-blacks, but reds must be potted only in pockets A or B (figure 95).

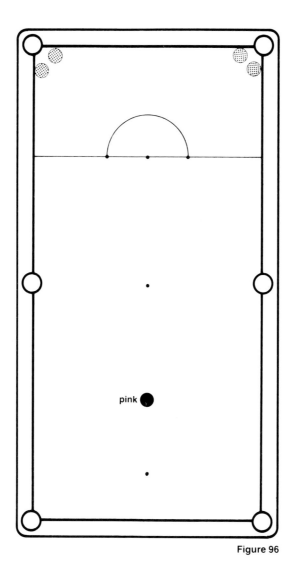

Figure 96

21. Pot four red-pinks (figure 96).

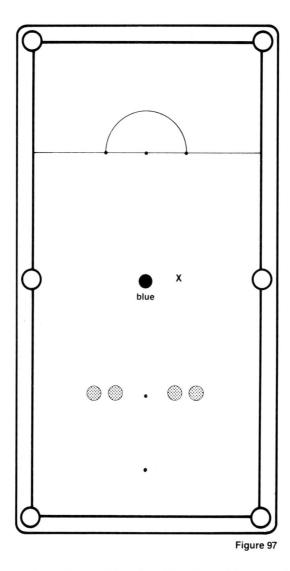

Figure 97

22. Place the cue ball in position X. Pot four blues and, with varying degrees of screw, stun and run-through, make four consecutive cannons on the reds (figure 97).

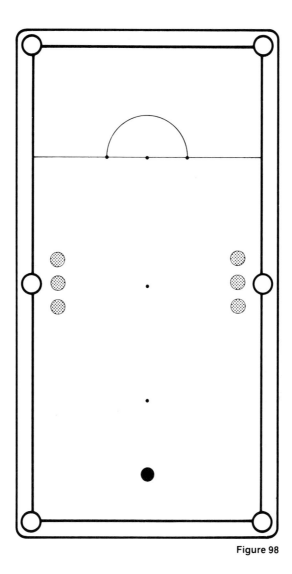

Figure 98

23. Pot six red-blacks (figure 98).

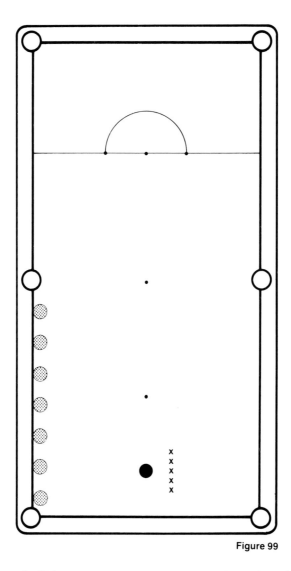

Figure 99

24. Place the cue ball in varying positions X to play plain ball only to pot the black and make seven consecutive cannons (figure 99).

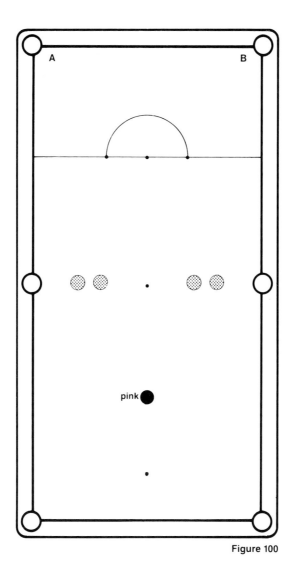

Figure 100

25. Pot four red-pinks, but reds must be potted only in pockets A or B (figure 100).

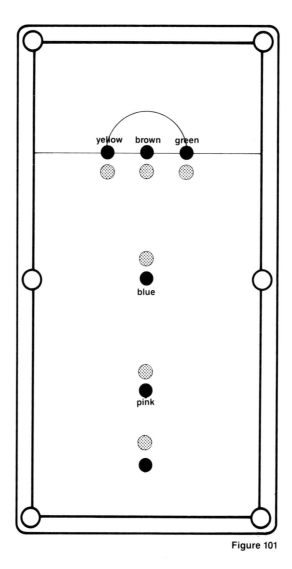

Figure 101

26. Clear the table by taking red then colour into any pocket you choose. But when you pot a red, the following colour must be potted in the same pocket (figure 101).

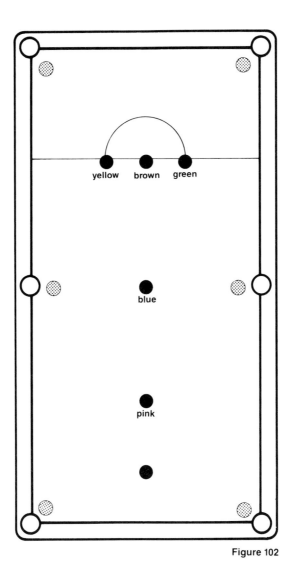

Figure 102

27. Pot red-yellow through to red-black (figure 102).

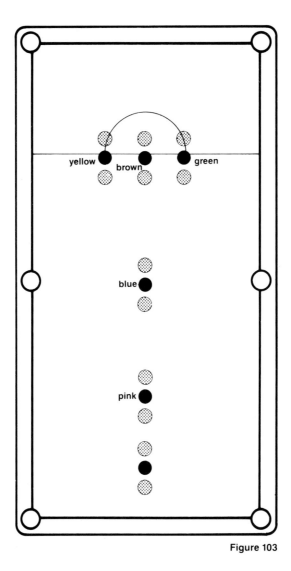

Figure 103

28. Pot two red-yellows through to two red-blacks (figure 103).

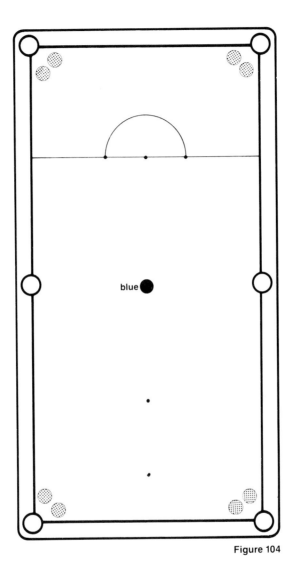

Figure 104

29. Pot eight red-blues, with blue potted only in a middle pocket (figure 104).

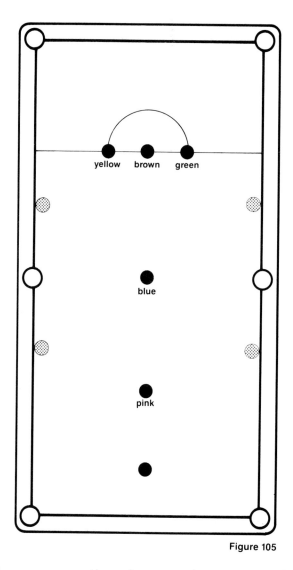

Figure 105

30. Pot the colours as many times in succession as you wish. The object is to move the reds from the cushions and eventually clear the reds. When a red is potted, you must take a colour (figure 105).

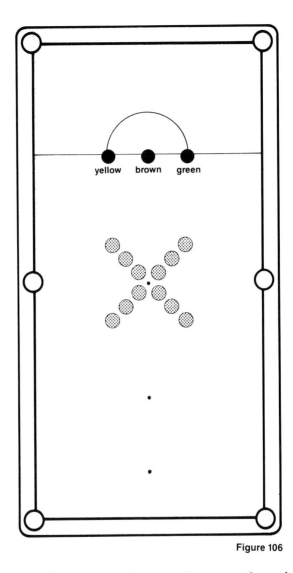

Figure 106

31. Pot three red-yellows, then three red-greens, then three red-browns (figure 106).

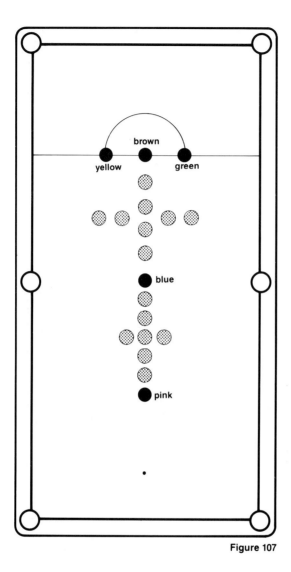

Figure 107

32. Pot three reds then yellow, three reds then green, three reds then brown, three reds then blue, three reds then pink (figure 107).

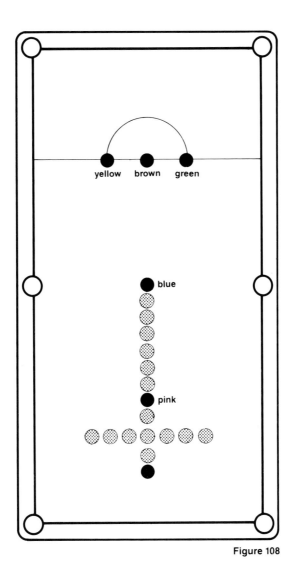

Figure 108

33. Make three century breaks (figure 108).

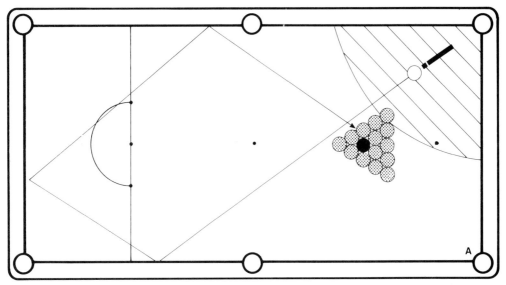

Figure 109

JUST FOR FUN: NO 1

This is a very pleasant way of learning angles and the pace of shots.

The object is to pot black. But black is in the middle of the pack. Remove a red from the middle of the triangle of reds and replace it with the black. Place the triangle in such a position that the black sits on the pink spot.

Place the white anywhere on the table, but you must come off three cushions — one of which must be the baulk cushion — to split the pack. You can use more than three cushions, but no fewer. Pick up the white if you want to after each shot and place it where you like. But it must come off at least three cushions.

Gradually manoeuvre the black into pocket A. Figure 109 shows the best way to do this, but it gets very difficult if the black strays into the shaded area. You'll have to adjust. It might look very difficult, but you soon learn about cushion angles and the speed of the cue ball.

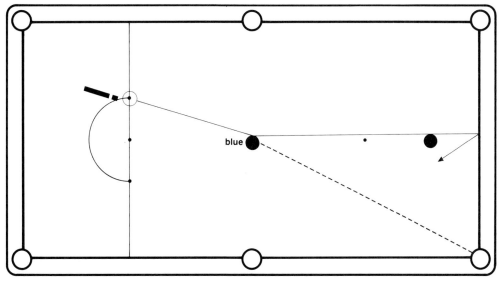

Figure 110

JUST FOR FUN: NO 2

I know a lot of pros who can't make the shot in figure 110. But it can be made, and it's a great teacher of correct cueing.

Place the white on the green or yellow spot and pot the blue off its own spot, into the top pocket. Bring the white up the table to hit the top cushion with side to play for position on the black.

This is an extremely difficult shot to play, as the cue ball has to be hit very sweetly or stun is applied. Any stun on this shot means that it fails.

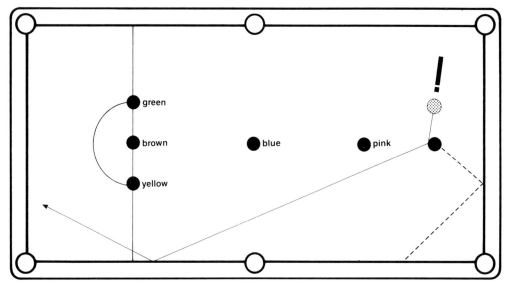

Figure 111

JUST FOR FUN: NO 3

With all the colours on their spots, as in figure 111, place a red as cue ball in position to hit the black and run down the table into baulk. Place another red on the black spot and play onto the black, wherever it has finished, to take this red down into baulk.

The colours must not be disturbed, and you must keep using a red from the black spot and striking the black wherever it lands. A lot of thought has to go into this, because you have to play the black again and again without snookering yourself.

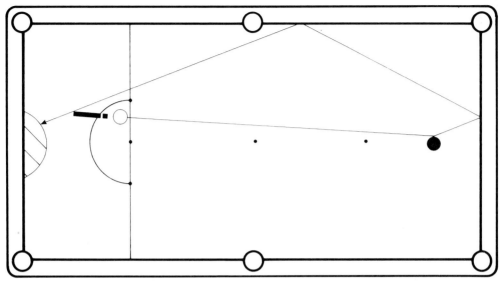

Figure 112

JUST FOR FUN: NO 4

Figure 112 shows a fun way to sharpen up your safety play. Mark a semi-circle at the baulk end, against the cushion. It should be about the circumference of a dinner plate.

Start with the black on its spot and the white in the D. The object is to hit the black and bring the cue ball back into the semi-circle. The black must not travel down past the centre spot, and you must keep playing both white and black from where they finish after the previous shot.

14

The Big Match

After many years of playing important matches, and watching others perform, I feel I'm in a position to pass on some thoughts about how to approach and handle them.

We all face the agonies and tension, whether our level is an inter-club league or the World Championship. How should I practise for the big match? How much 'gamesmanship' is acceptable? How do I cope with playing the reigning champion? How on earth do I keep my nerves from failing me? These are questions we have all asked, and I shall try in this final chapter to help answer them.

PRACTICE BEFORE THE DAY

The practice routines in Chapter 13 will, I trust, have helped hone your game and there is just one more thing I would like to add. If you want to know how to practise for the big match, I suggest you use a trait of human nature that is in all of us: picking faults with others (we have the faults too, but it's much more satisfying to seek them out in others and criticise).

Next time you go to your club, seek out the best players, the ones who are used to tension matches where something is at stake. Watch them practice. You will probably find that they play a lot faster and more slapdash in practice or friendly matches than they do in their important games.

Study closely and you'll find that their cue actions are faster, with less time spent on each shot. They also tend to play flashier shots. The deep screws, the tremendous shots with side and the smack of balls pounding the backs of the pockets are interspersed with over-the-shoulder comments on last night's soccer result.

There's nothing wrong in practising this way for the person who just wants to enjoy his snooker and play a reasonably good game. However, this is not the right way for the serious player who intends to win most of his matches and make it to the top.

There's no point at all in practising in this manner if, when you go into a match, you switch to a slower and more cautious style of play. What is to be gained? It only emphasises the difference in the mind of such a player that practice is vastly different from the big match.

The answer must be that every time you pick up your cue, whether you are playing for the table time or the national championship, you give 100 per cent to every shot. Use the same style. Feather or address the cue ball the same number of times as you would in a match. Stroke or hit the white with enough power to give you the position you need and not for the spectacular but blind-alley shot. In other words, play practice games with the same determination as you would an important game.

Winning snooker is built around consistency. This not only means the number of balls you pot and the size of the breaks you make, but also how you apply yourself at the table. The more you can remove in your mind the feeling that practice and 'the real thing' are different, the better your chances of cutting down some of the tension induced by feeling that you have to play differently when it's for real.

BEHAVING YOURSELF

This wonderful game of snooker will degenerate back to the grimy halls it came from, if we do not demand standards of etiquette from players at all levels. Indeed, you will find that conducting yourself in a properly sportsmanlike way can even help you stay mentally on top, because there is some satisfaction in knowing that, win or lose, you have not let yourself or the game down.

There is a saying that soccer is a gentleman's game played by hooligans and rugby is a hooligan's game played by gentlemen. Let's hope we never see snooker described as a gentleman's game played by hooligans. If we do not insist on standards, its public appeal will dwindle. I would ask you to:

* Shake hands with your opponent at the start of the match and wish him a good game — and sound like you mean it.
* Shake hands again at the end of the match and congratulate or commiserate. Have you seen the pros at the end of a match obviously discussing some aspect of the game as the final credits roll on TV? This sporting discussion is not entirely for the cameras — it's one of the ways in which the sporting side of snooker is demonstrated.
* Shake hands with the referee at the start and finish of a match. He is an important 'third man' at the table, and has a tough job. He is not your lackey just because he replaces the balls you pot.
* Never stand in the line of your opponent's shot.
* Never concede the frame or match when you have missed a shot. Wait for your opponent to have finished his play as the last man at the table.
* Declare all your own fouls.
* Never argue with the referee. If you think he has made a bad decision, ask politely if he is sure. If the answer is yes, thank him and sit down.
* Never volunteer remarks about your opponent's luck (or your lack of it) while the match is in progress.
* Do not strike matches, click lighters, shake sugar bags or cough loudly when your opponent is on the shot.
* Never complain about playing conditions while you are at the table.

A couple of other general points on etiquette: never interfere in other people's matches unless you are specifically asked to do so, and even then, think twice; and if you are outside a snooker room and want to come in, listen for the click of balls to signify that someone has completed a shot before you enter.

PLAYING THE OPPONENT

Imagine that you are drawn against someone who has a big reputation. Or perhaps against someone whose play you admired when your skills were no match for his, and before you improved to be able to play him on level terms.

It is very easy to be intimidated and perhaps a little frightened by this kind of opponent. This is where you have to train yourself to play to your opponent's skill rather than play to his psyche. This is one of the hardest things to do in snooker, but if you can get to grips with this, your game will improve many points. Let's take some instances to show what I mean:

1. Your opponent has a fluke which allows him to win the frame. You become annoyed and call him a lucky so-and-so, either out loud or in your mind.

Now you have made the game a personal battle. Part of your mind is on the opponent rather than on the match. The only place for your attention to be concentrated is inside the cushion rails of the table. This is the only place you can win the match. Keep your mind there, 100 per cent.

2. Your opponent misses an easy red and leaves you in, close to the black spot. There is an easy 40 break there for the asking.

In a friendly against Fred or Joe, you would confidently step in and strike gold, but with the reigning national champion hovering nearby and waiting to come in when you break down, every shot is a pressure shot. It is very hard to put an opponent of stature out of your mind while you are at the table.

3. You have a 64-point lead and all the reds are gone. Your opponent has no chance of winning, so why doesn't he concede?

Two reasons. First, he may feel that you are playing too well and that if he prolongs the game your concentration will wear thin, or you'll get used to not potting balls because he keeps leaving you safe or snookered. Second, he may feel that he is cueing badly and he needs to string the frame out to give him the chance to play more shots, hoping that in the process his own action will get into gear.

4. The opponent is a slow player, whereas your natural game is at a speedier pace. If he is a good player as well as slow, he can be very hard to play.

You might spend long periods just warming the chair while he compiles a 50-plus break, or you might go several minutes without having a chance at a pot. The frustration gets worse if he is also a good safety player, which most slow players tend to be. All this time spent on the sidelines and 'out' of the match means that your concentration is going to wander unless you force it inwards.

Narrow your mind so that you are oblivious to everything except what's happening on the table, the lay of the balls, the state of the scoreboard and the tactics you are going to have to use to swing the frame and match your way.

HANDLING PNT

I have no complete and infallible answer to the big, big problem of pressure, nerves and tension (PNT). But, again, a few hints might help.

Just as some people are born with the ability to jump higher, run faster, run longer, throw further or sing better than others, so some people are born with the ability to pot more snooker balls and cope with jangling nerves.

The first thing we have to do is to admit that PNT exists. This is almost impossible for some people to do, because they see this admission as a physical weakness, something like being scared of the opponent, the crowd, the occasion. When this kind of macho-at-all-costs person feels the tension rise, he concentrates too much thought and effort on concealing it from spectators. He might succeed in showing, at least on the surface, that he is not suffering, but it will add to the breakdown of his game.

I have never seen or met any player who doesn't succumb to PNT — and I've been around snooker for a long time. When you watch the apparently super-cool players on TV, you may find it hard to believe that I have seen some of them cry, be physically sick or not even turn up for a match because they couldn't face the thumbscrews inflicted by PNT.

So, for a start, be truthful with yourself and others. Next time you lose a match by missing the final easy black and people ask, 'How did you miss that?', be honest. Tell them your hand was shaking, if that was the reason. All you are admitting is that you are human. This is a big problem for many players. Face it, overcome it, and you can put aside any worries that your James Bond image is cracking.

I've heard it said that some people cope better with PNT because they play big money games and win more than their share, but this is not always the case. I have come across lots of players who can put it together when there is a big cash gamble at stake, but struggle to get into the second round of their local amateur knockout tournament. The reason for this is probably the fact that in a tournament, if you lose your first-round match you're dead. You can't bounce back and offer double or nothing. You have to go home match-broke.

I know there are a lot of people who disapprove of gambling. Indeed, in some of the countries where this book is being sold, gambling is illegal. I am not suggesting that you break the law if this applies to your country. As in snooker, you play by the rules. If a cash wager is permitted where you live, the fact remains that it can be a valuable way to get experience of coping with PNT.

There are some guidelines I would like to suggest so that you don't get swallowed up by the risks which come with gambling. First, make up your mind how much you can comfortably play for and afford to lose. Second, play just one match for this amount — this creates maximum PNT. The best of nine is a good match, as it usually takes a few hours to finish.

Try to play someone who is on par with you, in terms of both ability and wealth. The ordinary guy is going to feel more PNT playing for a tidy sum than is the millionaire. This gives the stockbroker snooker player a decided advantage!

Let's get back to the amateur tournament. The draw has been made, and you have got in as much practice as you can. Try to spend a couple of days before the match working out how you are going to tackle the play according to your present standard — and just as important, your opponent's. Is he a fast and impatient player who hates getting involved in long bouts of safety play, or is he the studious type who prefers to tie up the black, take a couple of red-colours and run for the long grass?

Think of the best tactics you can, and start with this plan of action clearly in mind. It must go without saying, but I'll say it all the same, that you might well have to switch strategy as the match proceeds. The fast, open type of player might surprise you by showing a lot of caution and safety — perhaps his potting confidence is off and you should attack a bit more. I do believe that a pre-match plan based on your opponent's known abilities is likely to be a worthwhile ally to take with you into the campaign.

Let's say the match is due to start at 7.00 pm. It's no good you steaming breathlessly through the door at 6.59 pm, asking whose break it is and diving into the match. The other end of the scale is just as ridiculous. You will do yourself no favours by arriving two hours before match time, with mental time to kill. You need to arrive at about 6.50 pm. This will give you time to let your eyes grow accustomed to the light, time for you to greet friends who might have come to watch, time to order a cup of tea or coffee and shake hands with your opponent.

You'll notice that I said order a tea or a coffee. Not alcohol. Strictly, not alcohol. I know a lot of players who say that a drop before the match helps them to 'relax' and release some of the tension. But for the player who aspires to the higher realms of snooker, this is poison.

Alcohol is only the same as taking a mild form of drug. If you are playing pressure matches regularly, the drug will need to be stepped up for you to feel greater effect. It doesn't take too long before you have stepped it up so much and become so 'relaxed' that you can't see the referee clearly! Seriously, I've known a lot of fine players who have ruined potentially outstanding snooker careers by drinking through matches. Alcohol can be a pleasant form of relaxation, but keep it well away from a snooker table.

While we are on the subject of drugs, I should say that there are players right now who use certain medications because they think these enhance their play.

One of these drugs is the beta blocker, which is used by people who have hypertension. It is a very good and commonly used drug for this purpose but can only be obtained by prescription from a doctor. Quite right too, as the only people who really need it are the hypertensives or those with chest pains.

It can make you feel more relaxed as it blocks your natural 'flight, fight or fright' responses and prevents you getting overly tense. I do not think it should be banned because people who suffer from high blood pressure genuinely need it. But it should be used only when prescribed by a doctor.

Another 'drug' is vitamin B. It's not really a drug, but it is used to build up your blood. What it really does is make you hungry. Some people think it creates a feeling of calm but this really is all in the mind.

I must stress that for the sake of our general health and for the sake of our game, we must put aside these artificial stimulants. Combat PNT by using your own inner resources. Only then can you say 'I' won the match.

Back to the match. It's 7.00 pm, you've shaken hands with your opponent and the referee, and you have won the toss. You elect to break. Don't rush. This opening shot could be the most important one of the match. Not only can it set the standard of your cueing and striking of the cue ball, but a bad one can let your opponent in for a 30-plus break. That is going to get him cued in, get his confidence soaring and set a trend for the match from which you might never recover.

But you make a good break, bringing the white off three cushions and leaving your opponent almost snookered behind the green. He plays an equally good safety in reply, leaving you in baulk for your second shot. The battle has begun.

You come to the table faced with having to play the first shot where you are going to really have to use your brains. I want to give you a checklist for every shot you are going to play, in this match and in all others in future.

1. Keep the same pace. Every player has a speed of play at which he feels comfortable. Some of us are hurricanes and whirlwinds, others are tortoises.

Keep your playing speed constant. Fast or slow, maintain the same pace. The fast player feeling PNT or playing badly is tempted to slow down, to deliberate more and feather a few extra times in the hope that this will make him more accurate. The slow player might try to speed up to establish some kind of missing rhythm (if you are this kind of player and find that it works, you might have to rethink your general speed of play and adjust accordingly). But generally, to change your pace is to invite problems. Be conscious of the pace at which you are comfortable and play best, and stick to it through thick and thin.

2. Pick your shot. It's all too easy to fall under the influence of PNT and allow it to rush your thinking processes too. Before you get down to address the cue ball, make up your mind completely that the chosen shot is the correct one. Failure awaits the player who thinks that red-to-black is the right shot, then gets down and at the last moment changes his mind and tries to screw off red for pink.

If any uncertainty creeps in at all, stand up and rethink. When you are sure, get down to make the stroke with nothing but the pot and position filling your mind.

3. Go for it. To suggest that you actually play the right shot at this stage of the book might make you think that I've let writer's cramp go to my head! But it is too easy in some game situations not to play the correct ball, because there is danger involved. Play the shot you must. In snooker there is always an excuse for playing a bad shot, but there is no excuse whatsoever for playing a shot that you know to be the wrong one.

There are few agonies to compare with sitting around after a match, trying to escape the knowledge that you lost because you should have gone for the long blue but decided to wait for an easier chance, then had to sit and watch your opponent clear up. Think positive! If the shot is within your ability and it is the correct shot, go for it. Go for it with all your concentration. It's a lot easier to stomach if you went down fighting rather than running away.

4. Concentrate harder on the 'easy' shots. There is no such thing as an 'easy' shot in snooker. But certainly, some shots are easier than others — and these are the ones into which many players put the least concentration. This is why so many 'easy' pots are missed.

Most players give the heaviest concentration to the tough shots, spending mental energy on ones with a 50-50 chance of success, or less.

It probably makes more sense to concentrate on the opposite, really focussing your mind on the 'easier' pots and getting perfect position after the pot. Play the 'easy' shots well, and you are likely to give yourself fewer hard shots anyway.

5. Keep your cool. It's easy to be composed when everything is going right. It's easier said than done to remain calm when things go against you.

Don't get angry with your opponent, the table, the noisy spectators or yourself if you are playing badly. It only makes your game go from worse to diabolical. Try to rationalise it. Tell yourself that you are a good player. Say to yourself: OK, I'm playing badly and I'm not getting the run of the balls, but I'm going to keep trying.

Snooker is one of those games where a match situation can change in a matter of minutes. Keep your composure and concentration together, play your way through the bad patch, and discover the great pleasure there is in turning a defeat into a win. Your practice, your consistency, your total mental commitment to what happens on the table — these are what will bring you through the black patches.

By the way, you won the match 5-0. (How could you fail with all this advice?) You play Steve Davis in the next round.